P9-CQM-953

In the
FOOTSTEPS
of JESUS

Bruce Marchiano

HARVEST HOUSE
PUBLISHERS
EUGENE, OREGON 97402

Design and production by
Koechel Peterson & Associates, Inc.,
Minneapolis, MN

IN THE FOOTSTEPS OF JESUS
Published by Harvest House Publishers, Eugene, OR 97402

Library of Congress Cataloging-in-Publication Data
Marchiano, Bruce
     In the footsteps of Jesus / Bruce Marchiano.
       p.   cm.
     Hardcover ISBN 1-56507-790-3
     Trade ISBN 1-56507-857-8
     1. Marchiano, Bruce. 2. Christian biography. I. Title.
BR1725.M3116A3   1997
277.3'0825'092—dc21
[B]   97-15530
                                              CIP

01 02 /DC/ 10 9 8 7 6 5 4

This one's for you,

Dad and Mom.

You're the greatest.

The list of folks who have supported, prayed for, and stuck with me through the production of *Matthew* as well as this book is huge. It's been a long journey, and may I say a great big "thank you." Without you all, it would have been an impossibility. A specific thanks to my family: Dad, Mom, Dennis, Lee, Nicholas, Dean, Melinda. Faithful friends and contributors Jerry and Mary Fischer, Teres Byrne, Mike and Dixie Gray, Mary Ann Jeffreys, Nancy Schmidt. Johan Posthumus and the *Matthew* production team. Rika Allen, Linda Fackle, David Seibert and Frank Schroeder. Betty Fletcher, Julie McKinney, and all at Harvest House. The people of South Africa, and the many folks, some of whom I've never met, who have kept me going with their constant encouragement and prayer. Again, thank you.

CONTENTS

985

116612

A WORD FROM REGARDT VAN DEN BERGH

Director, *The Gospel According to Matthew*

*H*OW MANY WRITERS THROUGHOUT HISTORY HAVE endeavored to document the workings of the one true God, to grasp the awesomeness of this God? Most of these works were written to satisfy the soul's yearning to know Him, as superlatives were heaped one upon another in an attempt to define and categorize Him.

God, Creator, understood by the human brain. And still the brain travails and the soul seeks satisfaction, until God speaks to us in these last days by His Son!

What a sublime experience to be called into such a working of God which you know no attempt of philosophy nor superlative writing can ever describe, outside of the power of that *testimony!* Here, within the pages of this manuscript, is a testimony which the Father in heaven wrote before the foundation of the world.

The people involved were created for the very purpose, and called for such a time as this—called to be a part of the ministry of the Holy Spirit, who is ushering in His glorious reign through the children of the Most High God. What a Lord, and how He loves us!

In *The Gospel According to Matthew*, we have had the experience of being led by the Holy Spirit through the Word of God as He, through His children, produced a film of the story of the Lord Jesus Christ as it really was. At this time in the dispensation of His era, He was making it a film that would reveal a joy in Jesus Christ of Nazareth that has never been seen before; and in the day-to-day experience of it, He would unveil to us who were involved such a nonreligious Jesus, such a warmhearted and loving God, as He multiplied to our hearts the manifold beauty of the Scripture, "He was anointed with the oil of joy, above His brethren" (paraphrased). The Lord further showed us that He would, as He did with the fish and the bread, multiply this joy of Jesus to the hearts of men and women, that all may live in that "perfect law of liberty." Hallelujah!

And all of this through a movie—a word-for-word film account of the New International Version translation of the Gospel according to Matthew. What a vehicle for God's anointing!

The awesome task of portraying Jesus fell to an actor in Hollywood only a few people had heard of—Bruce Marchiano. What a challenge to speak Scripture word-for-word and make it sound like colloquialism. Well, Bruce is a method actor in whom the method is God's anointing; and I believe he was chosen from the foundation of the world, born for the very purpose of playing Jesus, the Son of the Living God. There isn't anyone better to talk about such a grand encounter than he.

While we were filming *Matthew*, none of us quite realized what the Lord was busy doing—we couldn't see the wood through the trees. But now, in retrospect, we can only stand back in awe and give Him all the praise and all the glory for all He has done and all He continues to do.

This is the promise He gave us before we started shooting—Isaiah 25:6-9:

> *On this mountain the LORD Almighty will prepare a feast of rich food for all peoples, a banquet of aged wine—the best of meats and the finest of wines. On this mountain he will destroy the shroud that enfolds all peoples, the sheet that covers all nations; he will swallow up death forever. The Sovereign LORD will wipe away the tears from all faces; he will remove the disgrace of his people from all the earth. The LORD has spoken. In that day they will say, "Surely this is our God; we trusted in him, and he saved us. This is the LORD, we trusted in him; let us rejoice and be glad in his salvation."*

Rejoice and be glad, rejoice and be glad! The Lord will impart to your spirit His wondrous workings during our wondrous experience, and through this He will bless you out of your cotton-pickin' socks.

NEVER IN MY WILDEST DREAMS

PREFACE

May I never boast except in the cross of our Lord Jesus Christ.

GALATIANS 6:14

T HE DATE WAS JANUARY 23, 1993. I stared out the window of a four-prop AirMaroc plane into the black night of the north African sky. Cold and exhausted, I was on the final leg of a journey that had taken me from Los Angeles, California, to halfway across the world. In less than an hour I would be in the backseat of a blue Renault, whisking down a Moroccan highway toward a tiny, third-world town in the middle of nowhere called Quarzazate (Kwar-za-zot).

It was a town I'd never heard of, whose name I couldn't even pronounce. And though I didn't suspect it, it was a town that would launch me into the most remarkable, unimaginably humbling and wondrous adventure of a lifetime—a word by word, event by event, Scripture by Scripture, miracle by miracle walk in the footsteps and through the life of Jesus Christ.

I must tell you, it's strange for me to think about someone reading a book that came from my pen. Never in my wildest dreams did I even once imagine that I would write anything like this, let alone write it for others to read. But then that's pretty much the way my whole life has gone since I invited Jesus into my heart to be my Lord and Savior just a handful of years ago—one unimaginable adventure after another. Some of them have been great fun and some no fun at all, but every one, in one way or another, has been an adventure well beyond anything I could have cooked up on my own. And it is that one most particularly adventurous adventure—playing the role of Jesus in Regardt van den Bergh's film *The Gospel According to Matthew*—that brings me to this writing.

Now, it's very important to me that you know a couple of things from the start. First, there is no doubt in my mind or heart that this Jesus who walked the shores of Galilee 2000 years ago was the Son of the Living God, Israel's long-awaited Messiah. And I encourage any reader who may not share that feeling to go to the Word of God and take an openhearted look. You need not take my word or anyone else's for these things (that's how people get into trouble), but go to the Word of God and check for yourself. Only then will you be free to make an unbiased, uninfluenced, level-headed decision regarding Him and His meaning in your own life.

Second, know that I am in no way a pastor, teacher, scholar, or authority of any kind. I've never been to seminary or Bible school. In fact, I've only known the Lord as my Savior for fewer than seven years, and that makes me just a baby in Christ.

As far as incredible testimonies go, I've never been an atheist, built a financial empire, spent time in prison, or been raised from the dead (well, not literally anyway). I've never seen a vision of Jesus or had thousands healed at my touch. I lay claim to nothing so dramatic or grandiose. The truth is, I imagine I'm not much different from most folks sitting in the pews every Sunday. My weeks are more or less filled with the same stuff most of our weeks are filled with—working through day-to-day struggles and bearing up under day-to-day (sometimes it feels like hour-to-hour) hardships, challenges, and question marks. I suffer my share of blunders, enjoy my share of victories, and try hard to live and apply all the faith, seeking, and trusting that I can. But more often than not, it's all I can muster just to fall on my face and cry out to Jesus, "O God, I need You! I need You *now!*"

There is, however, one particular way in which I am soundly gifted— the Lord has surrounded me with a solid wall of "Aarons and Hurs"—

committed friends who support and hold me up through thick and thin. What a blessing! Without their constant prayer and encouragement, without their letters and reminders of God's promises, without their long-suffering ears and steadfastness—in other words, without all their faithfulness—it's doubtful I would have made it through the last six-plus years of life without one big-time failure or another.

A fax arrived from one of them just this morning. It reads, "My own life is being broken down to the bare basics at the moment, holding on to salvation; no special blessings or even promises—just the knowledge of being His child . . . having faith in God's *character,* that He is faithful, gracious, just, slow to anger, abounding in love, etc."

And that's exactly where I sit today—no spiritual giant with all the answers for victorious living, no bearer of astounding theological achievement. I've never even won a blue ribbon at anything, and in fact lost a spelling bee in the second grade by one word: banana (I added an extra *n*). It's important to me that you know this because we so often look at the writers of books, the guys giving sermons, the top-ten recording artists, the faces on magazines, the television personalities, or anyone shouting into a microphone and think, *Wow!* Well, let it be known, there's no "wow" here—just a sinner saved by grace. That's my only "wow."

You're reading a book written by an ordinary guy—an actor by profession—who, a handful of years ago, was quite simply blown away with the unique and extraordinary experience of portraying Jesus in *The Gospel According to Matthew.* It was a stunning honor, a humbling privilege, a breathtaking wonder—an adventure so phenomenal, words cannot begin to convey the marvel of it. Each day on the set was a lifetime of experiences and discoveries, every moment unveiling Jesus as I'd never known Him to be nor even dared to dream He was.

Before *Matthew,* I knew Jesus as my Lord and loved Him. But in doing the film—in walking through His life, in speaking His words, in putting my fingers into the eyes of a blind man, and more than anything else, in hanging on a cross—I fell *in love* with Jesus. Oh, who I discovered Him to be! A Man among men—joyous, dynamic, passionate, full of life; a picture of heroism, integrity, and truth—the Son of the Living God in every sense of the title; and His story is not merely "the greatest story ever told," but the greatest *LOVE* story ever told.

A few years ago, I was on my face praying in a Cape Town, South Africa hotel room. Just an hour away was the first meeting of a speaking tour that would take me into every nook and cranny of the country and put me in front of thousands of people, simply sharing the experiences and discoveries chronicled in these pages. I asked the Lord that night what He wanted me to do—what my purpose was in all of this. In the quiet of my heart, with my nose in that carpet, His prompting came: "Refresh the saints." What He did in people's lives in front of my eyes during the six months following that prayer was beyond anything that I dared imagine or anticipate.

And that is what has led me to putting it all on paper. It is my serious prayer that through the stories that follow, through my answering as best I can the simple question that I'm still asked every day of my life, *"What does it feel like to play Jesus?"* you, too, will be refreshed—refreshed in Jesus, the Christ, the Son of the Living God, who walked the earth 2000 years ago, living a very real life, and hung on a cross, dying a very real death.

As Hebrews 12:2,3 calls to us,

> *Let us fix our eyes on Jesus,*
> *the author and perfecter of our faith,*
> *who for the joy set before him,*
> *endured the cross, scorning its shame . . .*
> *Consider him who endured such opposition from*
> *   sinful men. . . .*

Consider *Jesus.*

Before we begin, please allow me the privilege of coming before the Lord in prayer. *Lord Jesus, thank You that You know us so well, so specifically. Thank You that You know every heart, every dream, every hope, desire, and circumstance. O mighty God Jehovah, let not one of us walk away without a fresh look at You, a fresh touch from You, a fresh understanding of You. Father, I submit us all to be loved, to be held, to be embraced by You. To be filled with Your joy. To hear Your heart and taste the warmth of Your smile. In Your precious name. Amen.*

PART ONE

FALLING IN

LOVE WITH

JESUS

In the
FOOTSTEPS
of **JESUS**

HOW DID I GET THE ROLE?

CHAPTER ONE

"Bruce, God has something really big planned for your life. I don't know what it is, but it's really, really big."

$\mathcal{O}$NE QUESTION I'M ASKED everywhere I go is, "How did you get the role?" It's a relatively short question, and I can tell that folks figure on a relatively short answer. But surprise—no short answers here. In fact, this answer requires that we first walk through a brief recap of my years leading up to *Matthew,* as it is all remarkably and intricately woven together.

Psalm 139:16 declares, "All the days ordained for me were written in your book before one of them came to be." It's a big one to swallow, that's for sure, but if you ever had any doubts about the truth of it, buckle your seatbelt and read on.

The year was 1976. Studying at California State University at Fullerton, I was living life more or less typically for an American college kid—lots of work, lots of fun, a lovely girlfriend, a great job, a host of good buddies, and loads of laughs. It was all one big day at the beach.

One afternoon between classes, I was sitting in the school cafeteria, chowing down my usual hamburger lunch and watching the world of academia pass by. Just the day before, I'd been briefly introduced to an easygoing history professor named Dr. Ronald Rietveld, and as I sat eating my lunch, he cut through the crowd toward me, a huge smile stretched across his face. In his hand was a brown paper bag and an orange juice, and much to my surprise he stopped and asked if he could join me. Having lunch with history professors was not one of my more common activities but I certainly wasn't going to turn him down, so I cautiously responded with something brilliantly impressive like, "Sure, have a seat."

Dr. Rietveld scooted into a chair, pulled a peanut butter and jelly sandwich out of his little sack, and then did something so extraordinary it strikes me to this day: He looked me in the eye and asked from the bottom of his heart, with a realness I'd never seen before, "How are you?"

A simple question—a greeting I'd heard a million times—but for some reason, looking into Dr. Rietveld's face, this "How are you?" was different. This wasn't just a clichéd hello or icebreaker; this was as if the man truly wanted to know if I was doing okay. It almost blew me out of my chair.

Don't get the wrong impression; I was by no means a lonely guy in need. I had a girlfriend who told me she loved me, a mountain of friends and family, and every one of them truly cared about me. But this history professor—I could see it in his eyes—it was as if at that moment I was *all* he cared about.

As you may have guessed, this guy loved the Lord, and as I sit looking back, it may have been the first time I ever "saw" Jesus in my life. His smile was full, his eyes transparent, and his care for me genuine and obvious; this tall, gangly man eating a peanut butter and jelly sandwich.

Totally disarmed, I met his genuineness by baring my soul, and in the process discovered I was not as fulfilled a young fellow as I previously thought. I discovered a good share of frustration—not quite fitting anywhere, trying to prove myself, and stumbling left and right.

After an hour, Dr. Ron told me where his office was, invited me to come talk anytime, then disappeared into the crowd. Thus, my first introduction to a true man of God.

I can't tell you how many personal crises I ended up spilling into Dr. Ron's lap through the countless talks we shared in the years following that lunch. He became my confidant and guide, never once turning me away, always meeting me with undivided attention and wisdom from Scripture. And though I don't recall ever actually confessing Jesus as my Lord, the seeds of truth he planted in my heart would sprout years down the line. Yes, Ron was a man in whom I was actually "seeing" Jesus, and it wasn't so much in what he said as in what he *did*—in the way he dealt with me and others. He just simply and actively *cared*—like Jesus.

Well, in my first year of graduate school, life came crashing down around me (at least that's the way it felt at the time). Remember that girlfriend? As my buddies would say, I was a "goner" for her—completely flipped and lost in love—and surprise of surprises, after months of ups and downs, she decided to move on, leaving me a heartbroken wreck.

It felt like I'd been hit by a Mack truck, and a day or so after it all came down, I reached for the phone to call Dr. Ron. The moment he heard the brokenness in my voice, he simply and firmly said, "Come over, right now." Rushing across the street to his office, I fell to my knees on his floor, shamelessly crying.

I will never forget what happened in that room that afternoon. Ron was standing above me, and as I looked up through my tears, to my amazement he was *smiling*. My heart was in pieces, and this guy was smiling! It was a strange smile—not his usual smile—but a smile nonetheless. Then, as if to add insult to injury, he opened his mouth and spoke two shocking sentences:

Bruce, God has something really big planned for your life.
I don't know what it is, but it's really, really big.

To this day I remember the look on his face and the tone in his voice—focused, certain, yet faintly quizzical. He wasn't simply encouraging me; he was making a point. And it was as if he were telling me something he didn't quite understand himself but nonetheless knew to be true—as if somebody very credible had whispered a mysterious secret into his ear, and he was merely passing it along.

Of course, in my heartbroken state I figured Ron had gone nuts on me. All I knew was that I hurt, and that was all I cared to hear or talk about. Besides, from my angle it didn't look as if there was any God at all, let alone a God who had big plans for me.

I didn't respond that afternoon, but I'm telling you, those bizarre words of his never left me. Somehow they took deep root in my soul and, as subsequent years passed, hung tenaciously in the corner of my heart, a constant whisper.

I specifically remember one sweltering summer afternoon in the mid-1980s. I was a struggling, stressed-out actor sitting in my car at the intersection of Hollywood Boulevard and Highland Avenue watching an avalanche of street people and tourists tread the crosswalk in front of my windshield. Waiting for the light to turn green, city sweat dripping down my nose, I had one of those moments when a guy is smacked in the face with the hard realities of a life that hasn't turned out like it was supposed to. I had so much potential—so much ability, so much support, so much talent—yet somehow life had become a red light in the dregs of Hollywood.

In the middle of that not-so-romantic reality, Dr. Ron's words flooded into my mind: "God has something really big planned for your life . . . really, really big." Something about it seemed so right, yet it was so starkly contrary to the reflection that stared back at me in the rearview mirror. I just sat there asking myself, *Did you miss it, Bruce? Did you pass it by? Did you somehow blow it somewhere along the line?*

Smash cut (that's movie talk for an abrupt scene change) to summer 1989. I had merrily skipped through the '80s, more or less guided by the standard pursuits of success and fun.

Interestingly enough, though not committed to the Lord, I was still sitting in church every Sunday morning (providing the guys weren't getting together for a softball game). I possessed a full vocabulary of Christian lingo and could "talk the talk" with the best of them. I was very aware of God and even prayed (especially when I found myself in a tight spot). If you had asked me at the time, I'd have told you, "Yes, I'm a Christian," but in spite of what I may have thought, I had no *relationship* with God whatsoever—a little religion, yes, but relationship, no.

That fact hit home in July of 1989, when life again came crashing down as everything I'd built it on was suddenly yanked out from under me. And when I say "crashing down," "yanked out," and "suddenly," believe me, I mean it. In May '89, I was a guy with $30,000 in his checking account, a devoted talent manager breathing new life into my career, and a stunning young actress neatly tucked under my arm. In July of that same year, a mere two months later, I was sleeping on a friend's sofa—no money in the bank, no actress, and too much of a wreck about it all to compete successfully in auditions. Overnight, life had all but fallen apart.

Thank God people were praying for me—people who truly *knew* Jesus in their lives—because one blistering summer day, broken to pieces, I fell on my knees in the hills of Coldwater Canyon Park, overlooking Universal Studios in the distance, and begged Jesus to save me.

I knew I wasn't going to make it on my own. I knew that only Jesus, the Son of the Living God, could snatch me from going under, so I cried out in desperation for Him: "Jesus, You've got to save me!" I gave Him my life—really and truly gave it to Him. A couple of weeks later, sitting in church, I felt moved to make it official by responding to the pastor's invitation and have never looked back. Praise His glorious name!

Two years later—Sunday morning, March '91. I was in my usual back-row seat at the Church on the Way, Van Nuys, California, waiting for my pastor, Jack Hayford, to begin the service. Thumbing through the bulletin, I saw a notice: "His Majesty's Players, seeking professional actors for a Christian theatrical tour of Australia."

This is great, I thought. *An overseas trip! With His Majesty's Players I can see the world and get paid for it! Oh, yeah, I almost forgot—and serve the Lord!* The next day I phoned the contact number and secured an audition appointment. *Wow—God is so good!* I mused.

The notice had also caught the eye of a fellow actor who, unlike me, had walked closely with the Lord for many years. As she casually talked about His Majesty's Players, a word slipped from her mouth that caught me by surprise. It was a word that did not compute with me in any shape or form: *missionary.*

Let me tell you, this was startling news. I don't know what to attribute my ignorance to, but when I responded to that notice, I was picturing pristine beaches and outback adventures. After hearing that word, though, there were two critical facts I knew 100 percent for sure—one, I was a professional actor; and two, I was *not* a missionary. I canceled that audition appointment as fast as I could get to a phone.

But as the days passed, I couldn't escape a nagging feeling that I was making a huge mistake. A still small voice, whose source I had no doubt about, seemed to continually lean into my heart's ear, "You blew it, kid." It trailed and cornered me everywhere I went.

More His Majesty's Players conversations took place, and more dirty words cropped up: sleeping in people's homes, raising money for airfare, "it's winter in Australia and they don't use central heating," performing for high school kids. . . . I would stand silently listening, smiling, and nodding, while my insides screamed in horror, *Are you people out of your minds?! Not a chance!* Still that nagging grew inside of me. Every moment of every day was overcast with it. It's a difficult thing to explain, but the Lord wanted me to join His Majesty's Players, and I knew it.

In the weeks that followed, I scheduled and canceled two more audition appointments, refusing to give in. You must understand, I was a very ambitious guy in a cutthroat, out-of-sight-out-of-mind business. For me to leave town for six weeks to do missionary work seemed career suicide. How could I explain it to my manager and agents? How could *they* explain it to casting directors? "No, I'm sorry, Bruce isn't available; he's in Australia doing kiddie plays about Jesus in high school auditoriums." Forgive me, but no thanks.

The Lord and I had raging bouts. I would be on my knees in prayer trying to shake Him, offering every argument under the sun. Finally, in frustration, I'd look to the ceiling as if into His face and explode, "I don't want to go!" And that was that—I just plain was not going to go.

Then one Wednesday evening I made the "mistake" of going to a midweek church service for the first time in my life. As I walked in, to my horror, an usher escorted me (the guy who always sits against the back wall) straight to front-row center, just a few feet from Pastor Jack.

Pastor Jack began his message that night by telling a story that took place when he was in high school. Among his many interests back then, football ranked high, and the biggest game of the season was around the corner. Young Pastor Jack was thrilled as could be and counting the days to kickoff.

There was one little hitch, though: He was part of a music ministry that was booked for an event the exact same day and time. There was no possible way he could participate in both. A serious struggle ensued within him between what he knew the Lord wanted him to do (to be faithful to his ministry commitment) and what he wanted to do (the football game).

For me, this story was sounding much too close to home, and as Pastor Jack went deeper into it, the Lord began tapping on my shoulder. In fact, He was tapping on both shoulders. Actually, He was *jumping* on both shoulders.

And as if that wasn't enough, the Lord saw fit to knock me to the mat with a right cross (no pun intended). Pastor Jack, explaining how he truly felt toward the ministry commitment, leaned straight at me and literally shouted, *"I just didn't want to go!"*

Can you believe that? The Lord was using my own words against me, and right in my face! I drove home from that service silently stewing. Parking in front of my house, I turned off the motor and convinced myself it was just a bizarre coincidence. Attempting to free my conscience, I risked a dangerous prayer: "Lord, I'm not going to phone the ministry director. If you truly want me to go (as if there was any doubt), have him call me. I will take that as 100-percent confirmation. But in case You haven't gotten the message yet, *I don't want to go!"*

You can figure out the rest of the story. Stepping through my front door, peering into the darkness, I saw a single, blinking red light—my telephone answering machine. I strode across the room and casually tapped the playback button: "Hi Bruce, this is Jerry Fischer, director of His Majesty's Players. . . ."

It was finally time to throw in the towel. Mighty God Jehovah was personally and blatantly giving me a direct command, and boy, did I know it. But in the days that followed, what appeared to be a miracle happened. Through the grapevine there was news His Majesty's Players was fully cast and didn't need any more actors. *Hallelujah! Time to return that call! Maybe the Lord just wants me to assist as a director, and I won't have to go overseas! Yippee!* I sauntered to the phone and confidently dialed. The conversation went like this:

> "Hello, Jerry, this is Bruce Marchiano. As you know, I don't want to go on this tour, and word is the team is complete, but the Lord has laid it on my heart (*a little Christianese there, to make me sound holy*) to phone and offer my services. Again, you don't need any more actors (*hooray!*), but I just want to be obedient (*it's getting thicker by the second*), so whatever I can do for you (*hopefully nothing*), here I am."

> Long silence.

> "Jerry, say something, will you?"

> "Bruce, two hours ago one of our actors quit. I've been on my knees begging the Lord to send us an actor; otherwise the tour will have to be canceled."

> Another long silence—but this time from my end.

There's an old African-American spiritual entitled, "*You' Arms Too Short to Box with God,*" and there aren't too many folks who'd argue with that one—certainly not me. I signed on with His Majesty's Players and went to Australia, kicking and screaming all the way. In just three months I found myself living what I'd tried everything to avoid—missionary kiddie plays and freezing in some stranger's spare bedroom on the other side of the world.

Pulling no punches, I can't resist sharing a little story about the tour's opening show. We were in this barnlike church hall that had probably been built sometime during the reign of Hezekiah. It was fully equipped with the latest in rusted folding chairs (some of which actually had four legs) and two space heaters that did a better job of taking space than giving heat.

In the first skit of the evening, I had to do a Three Stooges-type death scene, leaving me stretched on the floor, back to the audience. It was a very physical stunt, and lying there trying to catch my breath, I opened my eyes to have a look around while the skit continued behind me.

Well, right there, inches from my nose, was a huge dirtball. It was complete with hair, a couple of fingernails, and an unidentifiable, long-deceased, winged Aussie insect. With every inhale it slid toward me, and with every exhale it slid away—in and out, up and back, in and out, up and back. It was as disgusting a thing as I'd ever seen.

So there I was, never feeling more foolish in my life—a grown man, a professional actor, pretending he was dead and staring at a dirtball. It was one intensely glamourless moment, and lying there I silently mouthed to myself, "You're a long way from Hollywood, kid."

It was true—I was a long way from Hollywood. But as trying as it was, that tour proved to be one of the most wonderful experiences I've ever enjoyed. So much so, I'd recommend that every one of you give that missionary thing a try. It will be tough, that's for sure, but it will stand as one of your life's peak experiences as well—guaranteed.

Returning from Australia, I quickly learned that my career fears were warranted. My manager released me, saying, "Bruce, I think this Christian thing is going to get in the way." As she was my link to employment and progress, that left me seriously paddling upstream without an oar. Consequently, I spent the remainder of 1991 scrambling to find a new, effective agent/manager—a task not easily accomplished in the wilds of Hollywood—and as month rolled into month, I found myself more and more out of work, struggling, and, worst of all, blaming it on God. Every angry word of every angry prayer was underscored with, "So this is what I get for being a missionary!"

Thus began a season of life that was so crushing, it still knocks the wind out of me to think about. I spent the next *15* months struggling to find work and nose deep in all the despair and confusion that goes with it. My financial condition got so bad there was no option for me but to get a bread-and-butter job that would pay rent and put food on the table. It was a job that ripped my heart to shreds eight hours a day. It was a job that (and this is the key, though I didn't recognize it at the time) ripped my *ego* to shreds eight hours a day. It was a delivery job, driving scripts around town to producers, casting directors, and agencies—film industry professionals whose offices I'd previously entered as a professional myself.

Sometimes they'd look over their desks with silent eyes that said, "What happened to you, Bruce?" Perky receptionists who used to smile across their counters now reacted as if I had a social disease. Struggling through L.A. traffic, sweat pouring down my nose for five bucks an hour (my last day-rate as an actor had been $800)—without question, it was the most humbling experience of my life.

But praise God, somehow I stayed on my knees. Most of the time I was gritting my teeth, but I was on my knees nonetheless. And it was through no righteousness of my own; it was flat-out desperation. There was nowhere else to turn.

I remember forcing myself to get up early every morning to pray and read the Word before work. I remember praying my way through traffic all day long and even propping an open Bible on my dashboard in an attempt to memorize Psalm 139—anything to keep me from drowning. Coming home evening after evening, I begged the Lord for release, direction, explanation—anything. My mind was spinning constantly—*Is the Lord putting me through trials? Am I doing something fundamentally wrong? If God is so sovereign, why doesn't He do something? Yes—if God is sovereign, why doesn't He do something?!*

Little did I know the Lord *was* doing something; and though I couldn't see it, to other people it was clear as day. One afternoon a friend who was a veteran believer said, "Bruce, you're going through trials I don't see Christians go through for ten years into their walk. I've never seen anything like it. The Lord must be preparing you for *something big*, so hang on." As great as that sounded, and as much as those two words should have rung a thousand bells, I was too deep to hear any of it.

Finally things got so tough, for the first time since I landed in Hollywood exploding with passion and ready to take on the world, I began to consider walking away from it all. It was November 1992, and I'd reached the end of my rope. It was time to count my losses and call it a day.

That's just about when the phone rang. It was Jerry Fischer, the director of His Majesty's Players—the guy who had taken me to Australia on a missionary tour that had (seemingly) ruined my career—and the words which danced out of his mouth that indescribably miraculous day continue to take my breath away as I sit here years after they were spoken: *"Bruce, I got a letter today from some director in South Africa who's making a new Jesus movie. He's looking for a more down-to-earth, more real-looking Jesus. He wants a professional actor who's also a believer. I think you might be right for it."*

Yes, it was Jerry Fischer, the guy I never wanted to meet in the first place. What more can I say? Sitting here today, still in awe of the incredible ironies and the blazingly obvious testimony to the Lord's sovereignty, the uniqueness of His ways, and the "trustability" of His directives in all our lives—yes, yours as well as mine, as He is not a respecter of persons—I just have to stop and cry from the bottom of my heart, "Praise You, Lord God! So marvelous are Your deeds! Praise Your blessed name!"

On the other side of the planet, in a tiny, on-the-edge-of-civil-war country called South Africa, veteran film director Regardt van den Bergh was busy searching for a believing professional actor to play the role of Jesus in his most challenging and thrilling endeavor to date, *The Gospel According to Matthew.*

Regardt is a guy I like to describe as a slave to the Lord. He had been living a celebrity's lifestyle in the fast lane as one of South Africa's premier actor/directors, until he encountered Jesus Christ in 1987 and invited Him into his life. Regardt was *radically* transformed from the ground up. He'd tasted the Lord's saving mercy in such power and dimension that the former man was completely dead and gone, and the new man was not only passionately in love with Jesus, but sizzling on fire for Him.

When it came to the preproduction of *Matthew*, Regardt did all of his scripting, storyboarding, and casting on his knees, joined by his production designer, Bruce Rudnick, a remarkably talented brother in Christ. With Bruce at his side, Regardt sought the Lord in every creative decision, and I'm convinced what you see on-screen today is the direct result of those two in the many months before filming on their knees in that production office begging God to show them what to do and how to do it. There are several specific things about *Matthew* that just about everyone comments on as being of special blessing to them, and I'm telling you, each was birthed out of those prayer/planning meetings. It's as simple as that.

13

And when the cameras began to roll, Bruce continued in that praying/seeking capacity through to the end, unofficially serving as the chaplain on the set, daily bringing us words from Scripture to guide and encourage. He would sit in the background hour after hour, lips moving in silent prayer and intercession. It's a job he didn't get credit for, a job few people understood, but here's a trustworthy saying: It's a job without which *Matthew* never would have happened.

No doubt you're getting the idea I love these two guys with all my heart. How could I not? They had been praying for me long before they even knew my name, and now stand as my two dearest friends in the world. Surely you'll forgive me if I take a moment to say to them both, "I love you, my brothers. Praise God for your faithfulness."

Well, when it came to the role of Jesus, Regardt unwaveringly felt the Lord wanted him to cast a believer—an actor who knew and loved the Jesus he would be asked to play; an actor who lived in relationship with the Jesus he would be asked to portray; an actor to whom the Holy Spirit would have access. He was convinced that to do otherwise would be a fatal compromise.

Talk about a tall order! What are the chances of a film director in Cape Town hooking up with a professional actor who could carry a four-hour film bound for an international audience; looked about 30 years old; had dark, Middle Eastern features (by the way, half my ancestry really is Middle Eastern); was completely available during the busiest season of the year, and oh yes, knew Jesus as his Lord and Savior? Regardt was fast discovering, as his search took him to dead end after dead end, that his chances of finding that actor were slim to none. With just seven-and-a-half weeks to start date, the role of Jesus had yet to be cast.

The heat was on and Regardt was sweating bullets, but he knew deep in his heart that as the Lord had directed him, the Lord would provide for him. With that assurance alone he pressed on, as his now-desperate hunt took him overseas for one final search. It was December 1992, and his destination was first London, then Los Angeles, California.

As I'm told the story goes, with suitcase in hand, Regardt was bouncing down the stairs from his office, rushing to catch his international flight, when out the door came his production manager with a brown manila envelope in hand. "You might want to see this guy while you're out there," she said. He reached into that envelope and pulled out a photograph of one Bruce Marchiano, an actor from L.A. who'd given his life to Jesus three years earlier. Had she waited just ten more seconds, I wouldn't be writing this book today.

My life turned on those ten seconds, just as it did on that twisted-arm decision to go to Australia, on Regardt's obedience to the Lord, and on so many seeming coincidences and hapless, unrelated decisions over the course of weeks, months, and years that there aren't enough pages to contain them—all paving a path straight to *Matthew*. Yes, the God who created heaven and earth, who hung the stars in the night sky and measures every wave that laps the seashores of the world; the God whose "eye saw my unformed body while yet it was in my mother's womb"—this same God had ordained and appointed this day, and nothing in the world was going to interfere with it.

And here's the trick: He doesn't have any greater love or purpose for me, no greater sovereignty over me, than for anyone reading this page. His truth is true for both me and you—embrace it! Psalm

139:16: "All the days ordained for me were written in your book before one of them came to be." Glory to His blessed name!

———————

Downtown Los Angeles, Hilton Hotel, December 7, 1992. My pickup truck rumbled into the underground parking garage for a one o'clock meeting with some South African film director whose name I couldn't pronounce. A few days earlier I'd received a phone call from a London casting agency, telling me the director of this Jesus film was going to be in L.A. and he wanted to meet with me. So there I was, rushing to make the appointment.

Now let me ask you, what does one wear to audition for the role of Jesus? A flowing robe with three golden sashes? A halo? A white silk suit? How about a pair of jeans, flannel shirt, work boots, and two days' unshaven beard?

/Why would a guy dress like that? Some years before, a friend told me about a dream she'd had in which Jesus stood before her simply clad in a pair of jeans, a flannel shirt, and work boots. Now don't get scared on me—I'm not saying it was a divine dream from God. In fact I love to quote my pastor on these things: "Yes, it might be from God, and it might just be the pizza you had for dinner." But wherever that dream came from, there was something about it that really stuck with me—Jesus in jeans. There seemed to be something so right about it—something so genuine, so warm, so solid—*so Jesus.* And as I thought more about it, the obvious hit me: Of course, He was a blue-collar man, a carpenter, the son of a carpenter. His mother was a peasant girl. He grew up in a small town in the middle of nowhere. If it was America today as opposed to Israel A.D. 30, what would a man like that wear? You guessed it—jeans, flannel shirt, and work boots.

So there I stood at the concierge's desk of this fancy hotel, looking as best I could like a solid blue-collar guy, when a heavily accented voice belted from behind me, "Bruce!" I spun around, and for the first time looked into a face that over the next three months I would grow to love as dearly as any I've ever known—the face of Regardt van den Bergh.

He smiled. I smiled. We shook hands. We both smiled. I pointed to the cup of coffee he was holding. "Boy, I'd love a cup of coffee." Without batting an eye, he offered it to me. "Praise God!" I exclaimed. He smiled big—*really* big.

In that moment, Regardt will tell you, the Lord whispered into his heart, *That's the guy.* In the same moment, I will tell you, the Lord whispered into my heart, *You're going to be spending a lot of time with this man.* It was a moment so big—a moment that would take both of our lives and spin them around a corner never to look back, never to return. As we stood staring into each other's smiles, we stood staring into the face of an appointment from God, and we both knew it. Praise His remarkable name!

Regardt and I slipped into a conference room and chatted over that cup of coffee for about 45 minutes. He told me all about himself, sharing how he'd come to know Jesus as his Savior. I remember little of what I said, but all the talk had to do with the Lord, that's for sure.

The funny thing was, a woman was sitting in the room with us who I assumed was Regardt's assistant and a believer as well. She sat silently across the table listening as we two gushed on about what the Lord had done in our lives. "Praise Gods" were bouncing off the walls in free-flowing liberty.

A good 30 minutes into the meeting I discovered she wasn't Regardt's assistant at all, nor was she a believer. In fact, Regardt had just met her for the first time himself that morning. He didn't know her any better than he knew me. This woman was a Hollywood casting director who had been hired via Regardt's London casting agency to help him search for "Jesus." She was a film industry professional in front of whom no actor in his right mind wants his "praise God" bouncing off any walls! In fact, there's probably no quicker way for an actor to end his Hollywood career than to walk into a casting session roaring "Praise God!"

But the Lord totally surprised me. Generally, when one walks into a meeting like that, he knows exactly who he's dealing with. But Regardt was so excited, he overlooked formalities and introduced her simply by her first name. Had I any idea what her last name was, I would have known who she was, and for fear of it costing me work (I shamelessly confess), there's no way I would have let my talk fly so wildly. But it was exactly that liberty that confirmed to Regardt what he felt the Lord had whispered to him in the lobby: *That's the guy.* Let there be no doubt, the Lord is indeed very clever.

Well, eventually Regardt said, "I guess we should get around to auditioning." A few days earlier I'd been faxed Matthew 23:33-39, Jesus confronting Jerusalem's religious hierarchy, to prepare: *You snakes! You brood of vipers! How will you escape being condemned to hell? . . . For I tell you, you will not see me again until you say, "Blessed is he who comes in the name of the Lord."* Regardt couldn't have picked a tougher scene for an actor to audition with, and since he'd been an actor himself, I have no doubt he was well aware of it. Let me explain.

You snakes! You brood of vipers!—them's fightin' words if ever I've heard any. And therein is what makes the scene a challenge: There's no worse thing an actor can do in an audition than walk in and scream anger at people he's just met. It might be an Academy Award performance, but the bottom line is that people are people, and something like that puts people off even if it's pretend. But on the surface, that appeared to be what this audition called for.

On top of that, there was another problem, one that has no doubt caused most everyone who's read the Scripture a struggle or two. This is Jesus we're talking about—loving, gentle Jesus—yet the words coming out of His mouth here seem anything but loving or gentle. How could the two be married?

Have no fear—a solution was close at hand. When I first rolled into Hollywood in 1984, I chose a veteran character actor named Al Ruscio to coach me. Al's a great teacher, and having studied with him for years, I'd have to say he taught me pretty much all I know. But somewhere in everything I gleaned from him, he spoke a line to me that stands as one of the most valuable lessons an actor could learn. He said: "Bruce, every scene is a *love* scene. Approach every scene as if you desperately love the person you're dealing with. *Find the love in a scene, and you've found the scene.*"

It's amazing, isn't it? The Lord was preparing me to play Him years before I even knew Him. *Approach every scene as if you desperately love the person you're dealing with.* If that isn't a definition of Jesus, I don't know what is.

Hence the first mind-blowing revelation of the entire adventure was born as I sat in my house preparing for the audition, staring at that faxed Scripture and looking for the love. *Desperately love the person you're dealing with.* Unknown to me at the time, it was a cornerstone that would set the tone for *everything* I did while the camera was rolling in the months that followed. It was so obvious, so "of course." When it hit me, I remember falling back in my chair and breathing a hushed, "Wow."

Jesus loves people—*all* people, everybody, no exceptions—even these people He was yelling at. Sure, they were messing up; sure, there was sin; but He loved them—nothing could change that. So though the words were condemning, *the heart would be loving*. Yes, anger, but anger *born of love*—anger *born out of a broken heart*.

Yes, it was revelation, but practically speaking, what a huge chance to take in the audition! To characterize Jesus as a brokenhearted lover—I'd never seen or even heard of it. A statuesque figure thundering righteous wrath—that I'd seen; but an impassioned lover pouring out His aching heart—that was something very different and very risky.

But you know, it's a risk I decided to take. In praying about it, researching it, bouncing it off a friend I respected both as an actor and a believer—the more I looked at it that way, the less I could see it any other way. And underscoring everything was the simple fact that it matched the way Jesus dealt with me in my own life—straightforward, convicting, calling it like it was but *never* condemning and *always* loving. It was right and I knew it, so I decided to go with it.

In the audition room, I remember pulling out that faxed paragraph of Scripture, looking Regardt in the eye for any indication of reaction, and very gingerly putting it out there: "I've got a little different slant on this whole thing, Regardt (*gee, I hope I'm saying his name right*). I've been studying this, and I don't think Jesus was so mad, here, as much as He would have been brokenhearted." How confident I appeared, I have no idea, but inside I was swallowing boulders with every syllable.

Regardt remained stone-faced, soberly absorbing my every phrase. It was torture. When I finally shut up, he simply replied, "Okay, let me take a look at what you've got." I cleared my throat, looked into his eyes, and began speaking those words as best I could like a man whose heart was being ripped to shreds by someone he loved, "You snakes. You brood of vipers. . . ."

Regardt gave it the classic blank stare all the way through. I ended the speech, and after a moment of silence you could drive a truck through, he said what I feared most: "That was good (*usually a way of saying it was terrible),* but let's do the speech again, and this time show me righteous indignation. I want to see His righteous indignation."

My heart sank to the floor. *So much for my grand theories,* I thought, *but if it's righteous indignation this guy wants, it's righteous indignation he's going to get. Buckle your seatbelt, Mr. South African film director. And remember, you asked for it.*

I cleared my throat again, reared back, and literally exploded in rage, straight into Regardt's face. I'm telling you, I let him have it with both barrels blasting, "You snakes!" Taken completely by surprise, Regardt's eyes got as big as doughnuts, and he fell back in his chair as far away from me as he could get.

I ended the speech this second time, and as the dust settled in the room, Regardt just stared, frozen. Not a word came out of his mouth, but his face was speaking volumes—it was faint, but it was obvious— he was trying as hard as he could to hold back a smile. It was the kind of look from a director that an actor lives for.

Sensing the time was right, I rose from my chair and said, "I'll go now, so you two can talk behind my back." They both chuckled, we shook hands, and I slipped out the door. Closing it behind me, I hesitated long enough to hear the exclamation, "Wh-o-o-o-a!" What I didn't hear was the simple conversation that followed.

"That's the guy, isn't it?"

"Yes, that's the guy."

By the time I got home, there was a single message on my answering machine from one very excited Regardt van den Bergh: "I'd like to talk with you about doing the film. Please phone me back as soon as you can." I could barely believe my ears; I could barely draw a breath—he was offering me the role. I played the message back and listened to it. *Yes, I heard right; yes, that's his voice; it's him; he's offering me the role!* Standing in the middle of that tiny house of mine, staring down at the answering machine, I listened to it over and over and over. It was a freezing cold December day, three o'clock in the afternoon. Rain was pounding on the pavement outside, and this man I'd just met two hours ago wanted me to play Jesus—*Jesus!*

I wanted to tell somebody, *everybody,* but I was all alone so I just kept telling myself over and over, running it through my mind, trying to make it fit. It was so utterly inconceivable, but it was actually happening. The proof was right there on my answering machine—the director's voice—he wanted to meet with me. *Me!* He wanted me to play Jesus in his movie! I didn't know whether to scream or laugh or yell or cry or dance or fall on my face in a heap of thanksgiving. I didn't know what to do, so I just broke down and did it all. My dog must have thought I was nuts.

I went on like that for I don't know how long, and when I finally gathered myself to return Regardt's call, my hand was shaking so badly I could barely hold the phone to my ear. I was so afraid to believe it, so afraid he might have changed his mind, but it was the truth and he hadn't changed his mind—I was going to play *Jesus* in a movie!

That cold, wet afternoon my whole life suddenly made perfect sense. Every day without a job; every "not interested" look I'd seen in a casting director's face; every hot August night sitting alone, questioning every decision I ever made. Every prayer meeting I'd dragged myself to because it was all I had. Every Australian high school stage I'd acted on. Every girl who walked out the door, and every day in that delivery job. Every time I saw that "you're nothing but a dreamer" look in someone's eyes, and every time I'd struggled with the same look in my own eyes.

Yes, everything suddenly made sense—it was all a narrow road leading straight to the moment when I shook hands with Regardt. All of it—the against-all-odds choice to pursue an acting career, the specific techniques I'd studied and embraced, the semiethnic look that had left me so difficult to cast.

And the 15-month desert was part of it too. Every moment of it was will-breaking, ego-shattering, faith-stretching, independence-stealing—all necessary for the work ahead. First Peter 1:6,7: "Now for a little while you may have had to suffer grief in all kinds of trials. These have come so that your faith . . . may be proved genuine and may result in praise, glory and honor when Jesus Christ is revealed." Jeremiah 18:5: "Can I not do with you as this potter does? . . . Like clay in the hand of the potter, so are you in my hand." I was clay in His hands; He had to mold me into shape for the work that lay ahead.

Not so remarkably, I later discovered that Regardt had gone through an identical period of unemployment, and his was even more bizarre than mine. He was a well-known film personality, an award-winning actor/director, a national celebrity gracing the covers of the country's magazines. But for some unexplainable reason no one was hiring him to direct or act in a single film or television show. On the other side of the ocean, Regardt was struggling through hardships that directly mirrored mine. Our egos and self-sufficiencies were getting chipped away!

But, praise God, there came a day when the hardships were over and the desert sands gave way to cool mountain streams. And just for the record, that day was December 7, 1992—a wet winter day in Southern California not unlike any other; a day when the living God reached from the throne room of heaven, took an unknown actor—a truly foolish thing of the world—by the hand and led him into a promised land.

It was a promised land that would see the fulfillment of deep-seated, lifelong dreams beyond anything I thought possible. It was a promised land that would bring me into the sweetest friendships and most marvelous adventures a guy could hope for. And more than anything else, it was a promised land of such awe-inspiring value, such humbling purpose, such breathtaking closeness to the Father's heart that all the biggest dreamers in the world together could never have imagined it.

I was going to play Jesus in a movie, and in that, it was true what I'd been told through my tears so many years before as I knelt on an office floor crying over a shattered romance. It was true what had been spoken through the confident smile of a history professor named Ronald Rietveld, a guy who ate peanut butter and jelly sandwiches and acted a lot like Jesus. It was true even back then, long before I ever turned my eyes to God. To again quote Psalm 139 and again say it's not just for me but for you, it was true "before even one of my days ever came to be":

> *Bruce, God has something really big planned for your life.*
> *I don't know what it is, but it's really, really big.*

———————

The day after Regardt left that message on my machine, we had a three-hour lunch, went to a church service, and then sat in a coffee shop and signed contracts. I discovered that Regardt's poker face as I read that audition scene was nothing more than a magnificent acting job of his own. As I portrayed a brokenhearted Jesus, Regardt, though cool on the outside, was holding back a tidal wave of ecstasy on the inside. His direction toward righteous indignation had been nothing more than a director's trick to check the spectrum of my acting skills.

You see, months earlier he and Bruce Rudnick had been planning that same scene in their Cape Town office. As was their practice, the two men were praying before the Lord, begging Him to lay out the direction they were to take. Faithfully, the Lord did that very thing. He unveiled the scene frame by frame, and Bruce, the artist, quickly grabbed his pencil and sketched a storyboard. Thousands of miles away and many months later, completely unknown to me in that little conference room, I acted exactly to the frame what Bruce had scribbled on that storyboard. Regardt told me that as I was auditioning, he was completely astounded. The Lord was literally shouting into his ear, "That's the guy!"

Regardt also told me that after our meeting, though convinced I was the guy the Lord wanted him to cast, one thing puzzled him. This is embarrassing for me to say, but Regardt had personal reservations about my face. Exactly what they were, I've never been brave enough to ask, but leaving no stone unturned, he went back to his hotel room and took it to the Lord in prayer.

He told me that as he did so (forgive me that this sounds self-serving, but it's so significant a part of the story, I just couldn't leave it out), the Lord whispered these definitive words into his heart: "Cast the man's *spirit*, not his face." And so the issue was settled—I was cast. And all I can say is, praise God for Regardt's obedience.

———

The two of us said goodbye for the last time in Los Angeles through my open car door, late the night of December 8, as I dropped him off in front of his hotel. The next time I would see his smiling face would be through a dirty airport window as I stepped off a plane in Morocco.

Driving away, my eyes heavy with the lateness of the hour and the excitement of the day, I had no idea that in just seven weeks I would cross from life as I knew it to be into life as I never knew it could be. I would leave behind the ordinary and march far beyond the extraordinary. Though I couldn't begin to fathom it as I silently negotiated the Hollywood Freeway in my rain-spattered pickup that night, it was nonetheless true—I was going to play Jesus in a movie.

23

                         OLD MATTHEW
              They replied:

                         THOMAS
              Some say John the Baptist; others say Elijah; and
              still others, Jeremiah or one of the prophets.

          After a while, scanning their faces.

                         JESUS
              But what about you?

                         OLD MATTHEW
              ...he asked.

                         JESUS
              Who do you say I am?

          PETER gets up,

                         OLD MATTHEW
              Simon Peter answered:

                         PETER
                         (Quietly, emotion in his voice:)
              You are the Christ, the Son of the living God.

          JESUS stares at him, almost sadly. Then he smiles.

                         OLD MATTHEW
              Jesus replied:

          JESUS comes down to PETER, and puts his hands on either side of
          PETER'S face. MATTHEW looks from JESUS to PETER.

                         JESUS
                         (Gently, lovingly:)
              Blessed are you, Simon son of Jonah, for this was not
              revealed to you by man, but by my Father in heaven.

          MATTHEW looks back to JESUS.

          SCENE 170 OLD MATTHEW'S HOUSE.   DAY. INT.   170

          OLD MATTHEW stands behind his SCRIBES, dictating slowly,
          scrutinising their writing. One SCRIBE glances up awkwardly.

                         OLD MATTHEW
                         (Keen that they should get it right:)

PREPARATION—
THE CAMERA
NEVER LIES

CHAPTER TWO

Clothe yourselves
with the Lord
Jesus Christ. . . .

ROMANS 13:14

*B*EFORE WE MOVE ON, let me say that there are so many miraculous details, each its own little testimony, that if I told them all, this book would have to be published in volumes! For example, I was the *very last* actor Regardt was scheduled to interview. He'd seen everyone he could on three different continents, and I was his last possibility. If I didn't work out, he would return to South Africa empty-handed, just weeks before the cameras were set to roll.

His job, his reputation, the entire film, and every penny invested— all of it was on the line. The Lord took Regardt to the absolute edge (don't you just hate it when He does that?), yet somehow Regardt held on. What's that saying? "The Lord is never too late, never too early, but always right on time." In this case, in the nick of time.

But getting down to business, how does one prepare to play the role of Jesus? I can only speak for myself when I say, *on his knees.* I was very aware of the responsibility that had been dropped into my lap, and it was more than daunting. Never was a man less qualified to represent Jesus in this unique fashion (or any other fashion) than I was. Having never been to Bible school, having walked with the Lord

25

only a few years, I stood one unsophisticated, without-a-clue, entirely inadequate lump of clay who somehow had to get totally prepared both spiritually and professionally in seven weeks. Believe me when I tell you, I was shaking scared.

At the same time, however, I knew like I've never known anything that this was a specific work and purpose the Lord had for me—one my whole life had been leading to. In that alone I took this confidence: As this was a work He had for me to do, He would equip me with everything I needed to get it done.

Of course, that didn't mean I could sit on the sofa all day and watch "Bonanza" reruns—I had to do my part, so I stopped shaving, canceled my haircut, and hunkered down for what would be seven of the most intense weeks of my life—49 days during which I would pray like never before, study like never before, and memorize every word of Christ as recorded by Matthew.

To begin with, there were only two things going for me: First was the strength of knowing I was exactly where the Lord wanted me to be. Alongside of that—and this is so fundamental that if missed, the whole point of the book as well as the film will also be missed: I knew this wasn't an "actor-thing" or "film-thing" I was involved in. It was a *God-thing*. This was *ministry*, not a movie.

Therein was the golden key to my entire approach, the ground upon which every effort in preparation and filming would be built. We were dealing with God; not art, not drama, not business, not Hollywood, not anything but *God*. That meant getting prostrate on my face before Him, planning nothing in the typically prescribed way an actor would plan, and just begging Him to do what only He could do. I didn't want to make a single move or speak a single word while the camera was rolling that wasn't orchestrated by Him. It was of paramount importance that *His* Jesus get on screen—His and His alone.

And so my approach was simple: I did my homework, memorized the words, showed up on the set, and *prayed*. I prayed in preparation, on every airplane, in every hotel room, on the set, in the shower, and while brushing my teeth. I prayed before each scene and most times between takes. And pretty much always it was the exact same prayer: *Lord, make me a puppet on Your strings.* I can't tell you how many times I mumbled that plea.

Regardt had the same approach. He would pray, do his homework, map his shots, pray, show up, pray, pray, pray, seek the Lord, and then pray some more until the Lord gave him the scenes. And as the camera rolled, he would let the scene fly relatively unstructured so as to be completely available for anything spontaneous the Lord might want to do.

Regardt's priority was giving all directional power to God. He was not about to put on film any great ideas of his own, and neither was I. We wanted people to look at the film and see only one thing: *Jesus*. We wanted people to listen to the film and absorb only one thing: *the Word*. No great camera angles, no fancy acting, no dazzling effects—just Jesus and the Word.

For me, there was still a huge amount of work to be done as an actor: The script would have to be studied, each scene broken down, each relationship explored. But in preparation, the *real* work that had to be done—and this is bigger than big—was a work in Bruce *the person*. Somehow, in my heart, I had to get spiritually, soulfully, and in every other way prepared to represent Jesus. I had to get myself so out of the way, so cast aside—my own priorities, my own will, my own motivations—that the Spirit of God dwelling within me would be given free rein to shine in front of that camera as much as possible.

You see, the camera doesn't lie. Any film actor worth his salt will tell you it moves in on your eyes, picking up every thought behind them, exposing your soul to the world. It's the key to film acting. If an actor is lying, the camera will pick it up in his eyes, and the audience will see it and not believe him; it's just that simple. So it doesn't matter how good I may be at acting compassionate, joyful, loving—the traits of Jesus. If I am void of these things in my own heart, with that camera staring down the throat of my soul, I'm not going to convince a single man, woman, or child (especially the child!). So, you see, aside from the film, the key for me was to personally seek after what we're all called to seek in the first place—*Christ-likeness*.

For the first time ever, I began to pray prayers the Lord had been longing for me to pray, begging Him for things He'd been longing for me to desire: "Jesus, give me Your priorities and character. Mold my heart to reflect Yours. Fill it with Your compassion and love, Your graciousness and gentleness, Your mercy and joy, Your passion for

27

people and for goodness and holiness. Give me these traits in my own life—Your traits. Give me Your heart to serve and forgive, Your integrity and intimacy. Mold me into a man like You were a man so long ago. Yes, Lord, *make me like You.*" That kind of prayer became my constant heartcry and literally 90 percent of my preparation. I dove onto my knees and into the Word like never before, and the Lord responded handily.

It was a twofold process. First, in exploring what Christ-likeness truly was, it hit me that it was something I, as a person, could actively choose to do in my day-to-day life. That was a revelation. For example, "Love your neighbor as yourself"—a command straight from the mouth of Jesus. I discovered it to be fundamental to who He was 2000 years ago, and likewise fundamental to what Christ-likeness must be these 20 centuries later. In the past it always sounded like some lofty sentiment that would be nice if the world were a more perfect place. But for the first time ever, it hit me that it wasn't a sentiment at all, but rather a practical, doable *action* that could actually be *chosen* as a means of dealing with people on a situation-by-situation basis. I didn't have to take seminars and wait until my heart felt like loving my neighbor as myself (does that day ever truly come?), but I could make an active choice to *go out and do it,* in spite of my feelings. Like the Nike slogan, I could "just do it," and that would be the Christ-like choice—the choice He made daily, and the choice He would have me make.

But as hard as a guy could try to "just do it," sooner or later he'd fall flat on his face. And that's not to minimize the trying—it's like a sport—the more one practices, the better one gets at it, the easier it becomes, and the more fun it is. But what I really needed was a fundamental change in spirit, in character, in priorities; something (and this is the second part of that twofold process) accomplished only by the grace of God through the Holy Spirit. A supernatural, sovereign work of His carving Christ-character and cutting away gunk.

With that in mind, I dove to my knees, begging, "Change my heart! Fill me with Your love for people—for children, for old people, for hurting people, for angry people, for dirty people, for mean people, for unlovable people, for anybody and everybody!" Though I hate to admit it, I was desperate for the movie's sake.

Stuff began to rise in my heart, left and right. At times it was a strong conviction about someone from years past whom I hadn't yet forgiven. At other times it was a little nudge when some guy cut me off on the highway and I would start to retaliate. There were even things that went on without me knowing it, as I found myself spontaneously reacting to situations in ways I never had before. I'd walk away scratching my head and thinking, *Boy, that was different. Where'd that come from?*

Don't get me wrong here—I'm in no way saying that I am the embodiment of Christ-likeness and you'll never meet a more wonderful guy. Nothing could be further from the truth, and if you spent five minutes with me over a cup of coffee, I'm sure you'd wholeheartedly agree.

Listen to this one: Just after *Matthew* was released overseas, I met Sue Greally, who composed the film's musical score (what a marvelous job she did!). We were attending a gathering at the home of one of the executive producers, and as the afternoon progressed into evening I became increasingly aware of her "watching" me from across the room, as if there was something puzzling her. When things began to break up and it was time for everyone to go home, she came and said, "I've spent the last four months looking at you on-screen, thinking, *Who is this remarkable person?* But come to find out, you're just a typical American guy."

Ouch! A comment like that will bring a guy crashing down to earth real quick. Call me ultrasensitive here, but somehow "typical" is a word that doesn't feel very comfortable sitting so close to my name. Oh, well . . .

But on the other side of the coin, the day after I arrived in Morocco, having spent considerable time with Regardt, he looked at me and said, "You've changed. You're not the guy I met in L.A. a month-and-a-half ago." I wasn't exactly sure what he meant by that, but I knew he meant it good. Praise God for miracles.

Regardt repeated that kind of comment many times as we progressed through filming—"You've changed, my *bru* (South African slang for "brother"). You're a different person than when you flew in a week ago . . . a month ago . . ." I couldn't see it, but from his angle I was changing dramatically. Interestingly, in watching *Matthew* today and remembering the sequence of scenes as they were shot, I can see it as plain as day—the "Jesus" in scenes filmed toward the end of the shoot is light years beyond the "Jesus" in scenes filmed early.

But of course—I was literally spending 15 hours a day speaking and walking through the Word of God. It's "living and active and sharper than any two-edged sword," and I was neck-deep in it, all day, every day—how could a human being possibly *not* change?

––––––––––––––

The Word of God—in those seven weeks of preparation, I literally spent all day and night soaked in it. Early mornings were given to general, personal reading, then it was straight into the Gospel—studying, researching, breaking down the events into filmic scenes, and perhaps most significantly, memorizing every word Jesus spoke as recorded by Matthew.

A good six hours-plus every day went into that memorizing. I will never forget the cold December morning I first sat at my desk and opened a paperback New Testament to Matthew 5—the Sermon on the Mount. It seemed my biggest challenge, so I wanted to tackle it as quickly as possible. "Blessed are the poor in spirit, for theirs is the kingdom of heaven. Blessed are those who mourn, for they will be comforted. Blessed . . ."

It was a tremendous undertaking. Everything I would say while that camera was rolling had to be word-for-word, spot-on, every "if," "and," and "but"—not a syllable added or deleted. There was literally zero margin for error, as nothing other than the exact text would be acceptable—that was the intent of the whole film and the essential requirement of the licensing agreement from the International Bible Society: to literally *be* the Word of God in the Gospel of Matthew in its entirety. When we got on the set and the camera rolled, at my slightest mistake it would be, "Cut! Set up for another take," so this memorizing was critical.

I can't tell you the countless hours and days, repeating and repeating and repeating till it was all solidly in my head. And I can't tell you how God met me in the task with incredible grace. That first day I learned only a few paragraphs, but as weeks went on, entire pages began to stick in a single setting. Eventually I worked to where I could start with Jesus' first sentence, "Let it be so now; it is proper for us to do this to fulfill all righteousness," and without stopping, whip all the way through to "And surely I am with you always, to the very end of the age." I'd do it over and over, rattling it off like an auctioneer, reciting all through the day while working out, doing laundry, running my dog, pouring a cup of coffee—"Let it be so now . . . to the very end of the age."

It was of the utmost importance that the words become entirely second nature to me. Only then would my mind be free to concentrate on Jesus' *behavior* and *actions* toward others. Only then would I be free to fully and actively love people as Jesus undoubtedly did.

Another unique challenge faced me with regard to the words. They're the most significant pearls of truth ever spoken, but 2000 years ago, in the context of the realities in which they were spoken, it was simply Jesus—a very real person—talking with very real people. In the moment when Jesus said, "It is not the healthy who need a doctor, but the sick," He wasn't pontificating edicts for generations to come but looking into the eyes of a specific human being, having a face-to-face conversation with him. He was simply Jesus—simultaneously man and Son of God—answering a simple question. Bringing the words "down to earth" to that human, colloquial level was a critical thing for me to grab hold of and present on-screen, so critical that Regardt and I had lengthy discussions about its importance and the challenge it would present.

It was seven solid weeks of Word, Word, and more Word. To my eyes, it seemed nothing more than a Mount Everest to climb with little time to climb it in, but the Lord was no doubt looking through a different set of eyes. Let me sidestep and tell a quick story . . .

I had never been one to memorize Scripture, but as I quoted earlier, "The word of God is living and active and sharper than any two-edged sword." I have a feeling that in God's economy, as *my* motive was purely for the film, *He* was having me memorize for the purpose of changing my heart.

Point in fact, an odd thing happened with regard to my receiving a copy of the final script from the Cape Town production office. The way the film was structured, some of the Jesus dialogue would be narrated by old apostle Matthew, and I was anxious to get my hands on the final draft so I wouldn't "waste" time memorizing those sections. A copy was express-posted to me immediately upon being cast, but mysteriously, it never arrived. As day turned into precious day, I found myself with no choice but to cover my bases and memorize everything.

No sooner did I have it all down when, just as mysteriously, the script arrived. Gee, thanks! I had done far more work than I needed, and I wasn't too happy about it. But on the set I quickly realized that the Lord had a whole different preparation plan than I did. In *His* economy, what I needed was a heart-change more than anything else, and He knew that memorizing all that Word was vital in providing it. What seemed to me misspent time was to Him the optimal use of my time. By witholding that script, He "tricked" me into doing what He knew was best. Amazing!

And I'll tell you, it worked. I can't begin to list the times I've been in a situation and one of those Scriptures I'd memorized unwittingly would rise to the surface of my heart; sometimes convicting, sometimes encouraging, sometimes just giving a tender nudge in my spirit. Yes, I've become a big fan of memorizing the Word. As the saying goes, "You are what you eat," so feast on it, friend, and enjoy!

Drawing close to Jesus and memorizing His words—that was all great and wonderful, but there was also research to be done. I picked up a trusted study on the Gospel of Matthew, borrowed a book that gave a peek into the original Greek language it was written in, and sat down to gain a historical/cultural framework as well as a basic understanding of what I call "the big picture"—the spiritual dynamics of the events recorded.

Were my eyes ever blasted wide! As the books cracked and the pages unfolded, a whole world opened up that I never knew existed, the world of first-century Israel: its people, its priorities, its traditions, its expectations, its confusions, its politics . . . And when it came time to investigate the original Greek words—whoa! What a night-and-day difference! I made so many discoveries, I don't know where to begin.

One example that springs to mind is Jesus' teaching on divorce: "Anyone who divorces his wife, except for marital unfaithfulness, and marries another woman commits adultery." My study showed that divorce was a very hot issue at the time, giving rise to scores of debates and much controversy. When Jesus chose to speak openly like that, He was going on public record and putting Himself out on a limb. In voicing such a cut-and-dried position, one way or the other He was bound to offend a lot of people and most certainly lose fans and followers.

Here's the rub: Jesus undoubtedly knew well that He was walking into a hornet's nest and His words were going to blast holes in His popularity rating, yet He marched in and spoke them anyway. I don't know how that simple reality strikes anyone else, but the first time I saw it, it spoke volumes to me about the kind of man Jesus was 2000 years ago; and that was the treasure I needed to uncover—*the kind of a man Jesus was.*

It told me He was anything but a popularity-seeking, politic-playing, people-pleaser; rather, He was a man who told it like it was, regardless of the inevitable consequences to His own life. It told me He was a man of courage and integrity, a man who stood alone for what was right no matter the personal cost. It told me He was very *heroic.*

You see, in those days, all a guy had to do to get divorced was give his wife a piece of paper stating that intent and boot her out the door—a convenience that more or less reduced women to a status lower than livestock. The men, of course, absolutely loved it. For them it was an ideal arrangement, one they handily interpreted the law of Moses to allow for.

Along comes Jesus who blows their self-serving hypocrisy out of the water by looking them in the eye and basically saying, "No, you can't do that anymore." He was taking a radically unpopular stand on a sizzling hot issue, risking their misunderstanding Him to undermine the Law, saying that women are people too and that the Father loves them as much as He loves anybody, and you just can't treat them like that and expect to get away with it.

Can you imagine the shock waves He must have caused that day? Can you imagine the silence that must have fallen over the crowd? Can you imagine the tension at many a supper table that evening as husbands sat stewing while their wives sat across from them grinning? Ah, what a day it must have been for the ladies!

So you see, what many perceive as an unsympathetic Jesus making hardline demands by teaching what most people wish wasn't in the Gospel (being perfectly honest with ourselves) suddenly took on new meaning to me. Suddenly I saw a Jesus who was not so much unsympathetic but rather of uncompromising principle, standing alone for truth and liberating the oppressed, a Jesus who willingly took an unpopular stand for His Father's heart, His Father's will, and for His Father's daughters—fully aware it would cost Him not only friends and followers, but ultimately *His life*. Wow! Surely you must agree, *that's quite a man!*

Jesus—the man. My final leg of preparation took me on another journey through the Gospel with an entirely different focus. I necessarily approached it as an actor looking at a script. After all, that's what my script was—the Gospel—and it was my job to break it down on a scene-by-scene basis, analyzing each one as in any other screenplay.

What a difficult mindset for me as a believer to get into! For lack of a more proper way to phrase it, in this particular study I essentially had to divorce myself from my Christian thinking in terms of life-truths and examine each event in light of its practical, on-the-day realities and personal relationships.

Are you getting an idea of the complexity of my preparation? On the one hand, I had to draw desperately close to Jesus as my Lord and Savior, and on the other, explore Him as the human being He was 2000 years ago. On the one hand, I had to comb the Gospel for spiritual truth, and on the other, focus on its simple, first-century realities. How it all got kept straight and woven together, only the Holy Spirit knows.

Now, let me see if I can explain an actor's approach to Jesus. This is big, so pour a cup of coffee and settle in. We're cookin' now, folks!

How does one "play" Jesus? Tough question, tough job; but it was mine to answer and mine to do. Sitting down to build an approach, I knew only one thing for sure—a reality so unarguable, so fundamental, I never once questioned it: *I couldn't play God*. End of story.

The way I saw it, absolutely no one—not Robert De Niro, Al Pacino, and Dustin Hoffman combined (sorry, guys) could even begin to scratch the surface of that one. Beyond that, the script was solidly the Word of God, so as far as I was concerned, God was taken care of. He surely would need no help from me, and I wasn't about to mess with it by trying to convey some pious sense of "God-ness" or some religious façade of what I thought holiness might look like. Any approach like that would have proven silly at best.

Another thing—and this is a huge thing—from day one Regardt said something that would serve as a plumb line for everything we studied and did: "Bruce, I believe the Lord wants us to film the *reality* of Jesus Christ as opposed to the 'religion' of Him." Our prayer would not be, "Lord, show us how to make this look beautiful and fantastic," but rather, "Lord, show us how to make this look *the way it was*." Reality was a prime directive.

So, for me to play God was simply out of the question. But there was one thing I could do, and it was directly in accord with Regardt's mandate: I could explore the personality and character of Jesus, *the man.* I could look at the things Jesus did, the choices He made, the realities He walked in (an actor's analysis), and ask the question, "What does this all tell me about the kind of man Jesus was 2000 years ago?"

Realities. . . . There is a specific image of first-century Jesus I'd dare say most folks have ingrained in their minds. It's the image I grew up believing, and in speaking to people around the world, I've learned how common an image it is. It's of a serene, mystical figure: manicured hands, perfectly combed hair, cascading white robes, rosy cheeks, arms stretched wide, gaze fixed heavenward, baritone-voiced, and divinely aloof.

Now, as lovely as that may appear, one of my first and most significant discoveries was that reality was very different. Jesus was a real person living a real life, and everything around Him was real as well. "The kingdom of heaven is like a mustard seed, which a man took and planted in his field. . . ." As He spoke those words, there had to have been babies crying, people coming and going, donkeys braying, camels doing whatever camels do, and a whole mishmash of other first-century activities going on all around Him. I remember, in several of the scenes we shot, being interrupted by those very things and distinctly thinking, *Wow, this had to have happened to Jesus* (and He didn't have the benefit of a second take!).

I remember as well when we filmed the feeding of the 5000. What a glorious experience it was! The day was steaming hot, the crowd was 2500 strong, complete with children, animals, and every other first-century effect the art department could come up with. The cameras rolled and I coursed through the throngs, stopping to heal a lame man who was lying in the dirt—he hugged and hugged me in thanksgiving. John the Beloved belly-laughed, and we each threw an arm around the other. Little ones were thrust into my embrace left and right. An old woman took my face and kissed me with all she had. A basket of loaves and fishes was laid in my hands. "Cut!" Regardt yelled above the excitement.

After an hour, a look in the mirror showed sweat tumbling down my neck, robes soiled from top to bottom, hair a windblown mess, face dark and weathered—believe me, I was anything but glowing and rosy-cheeked. Our makeup artist took one glance and threw his arms up in surrender.

But you know, it really hit home that remarkable day—that's the way it must have been 2000 years ago. It was real life, and it wasn't the pretty side of life. It was people, and people were poor, hungry, oppressed; emotions were running high; there was excitement, celebrating, laughter, and weeping; the sun was beating down, the wind was blowing, and every broken heart and sick body for miles was pressing in on their newfound hero—Jesus.

I'll never forget the smell of sunbaked humanity and the dribble of infants I'd held overtaking my robes. Field dust and mud was caked between my toes. My face and arms were glazed with soil, sweat, and hard sun. It was not a pretty picture, but undoubtedly a picture resembling first-century Jesus as He moved among crowd upon crowd, day after day.

One afternoon while we were filming, a sandal strap broke and I sat on a stump to fix it. There I was working this strip of tired leather into a fresh knot, and it hit me—Jesus could raise people from the dead, He could feed thousands with a handful of scraps, He could walk across a stormy sea, *yet He repaired His sandals with His own two hands.* I looked at the dirt under my fingernails, and thought, *Jesus.* I'm telling you, I was overcome with emotion—it was so simple, so basic, so shockingly right. I rushed to tell Regardt. He just nodded in awed silence.

We would weave that into our next shot—one of my favorite scenes in the film—Jesus telling Peter to go fishing for the temple tax. Here was clumsy Peter, so perplexed and full of doubt; and here was the Son of God sitting quietly in a doorway, enjoying the breeze, repairing His well-worn sandal in preparation for the journeys ahead. Wow!

These are the kinds of very simple, very real, yet largely overlooked details that were explored and discovered. It was my homework, and a great pleasure, to be sure. Somehow through it all Jesus became so intensely real, so much more tangible, so much more lovely and breathtaking, so much more glorious and awesome—so much more God.

Quick acting lesson: the makeup of a man is in his actions—in what he *does.* So when an actor approaches a character, he grabs the script (in my case, the Gospel) and looks at what the character *does,* asking the question, "*Why* would he choose to do that, as opposed to anything else he could have done? What does it say about the character's priorities and motivations—about the character's *heart?*"

Well, right off the bat there's a huge discovery (at least to me). It's something that hadn't before occurred to me, and it spun my head around in startling realization: *Jesus had a choice.* I'd never thought about it before, but I always had a concept of Jesus just automatically blazing through His Father's will, fulfilling Scripture, doing a miracle here and there, all the way to Calvary, thank you very much.

But, you know, if anybody had a choice in life, it was the Son of the Living God. No one was forcing Him to do the things He did. He *chose* to obey His Father every step of the way. I don't know how that strikes anyone else, but to me it was big-time revelation.

So, in preparation, I had to look at every Gospel story, piece out the things Jesus did, and ask, "Why choose that?" in the context of the specific circumstances and human dynamics He was involved in. Let me give you a quick example—it's a story we'll explore in detail later, but it's too good to pass here.

This is the scene: Jesus stands on trial before Pilate. False accusations are flying at Him, the crowd is screaming for blood, and Pilate is trying desperately to let Him off the hook. According to Matthew, Jesus stands silently amid all this, doing/saying only one thing, "Yes, it is as you say." With all the power of heaven and earth at His fingertips, with all the options in the universe, He chooses to do nothing but speak that one line.

Now, from my angle, that is definitely *different* behavior. It points to a vastly different kind of person—a man with vastly different priorities and a whole different "why" steering His actions and governing His behavior. It points to a man with one vastly different *heart*—Jesus.

Before I could blink twice, I was staring at January 23, 1993. I had worn my knees raw praying, my paperback Gospel thin studying, and my brain cells dry memorizing. Seven intensive, round-the-clock weeks had been logged, and I didn't have the slightest idea if any of it was going to work. But it was much too late to think about that—I'd believed what I'd believed, studied what I'd studied, prepared what I'd prepared, done what I'd done . . . and the day to see if it was all going to fly had arrived.

I walked into Los Angeles International Airport, slimmed down, beefed up, tanned, long-haired, and bearded. My suitcase contained three pair of Levi's, some favorite T-shirts, running shoes, script, notes, books, tapes, and a Bible. My soul was full of the words of Christ, and my hand gripped a Swissair business-class ticket from Los Angeles to Zurich, to Casablanca, to Quarzazate, to Cape Town, and back to L.A. I stood in the middle of that busy terminal and joined hands with my parents and two dear friends. We prayed and hugged, then I slipped between the metal detectors, turned for a final wave, and disappeared through the tunnel, all the while my heart pounding out of my chest like thunder.

It was as if I'd passed through the gates of paradise, though at the time I was much too scared and in shock to even realize it, let alone enjoy it. I remember watching myself go through the motions: "Passport, please"; "Boarding pass, please"; "Enjoy your flight, Mr. Marchiano." (*Wow! She called me Mr.!*) Trying my best to appear cool and as if I did this every day of my life, I was screaming on the inside, half in excitement and half in terror.

The guy seated next to me was an ambassador from Italy. He was wearing a suit, and the flight attendant spoke perfect Italian to him. I was wearing jeans and a T-shirt, and she just giggled at me.

The ambassador showed me how to use my footrest—I couldn't find the button to release it. He smiled over his newspaper and in a thick, exotic accent casually asked, "For what are you going overseas?"

I sat staring past him for what felt like an hour, then heard myself speak a sentence that I could hardly believe was coming out of my mouth. It was a sentence that in my wildest imaginings I could never have conceived uttering. It was a sentence so extraordinary, so unfathomably magnificent, it couldn't possibly be the truth—it couldn't possibly be real. But it was real, it was the truth, and I was living it:

I'm an actor, and I'm flying to Morocco to play the role of Jesus in a new film, *The Gospel According to Matthew*.

Last night a friend reminded me of a conversation we'd had just a week before boarding that jet and uttering those words. She'd asked, "How does it feel to be the one guy in all the world that God chose to portray Him in this film?" I had no memory of it, but as she tells the story, I simply shrugged my shoulders and answered, "Beats me." And there you have it—it was just too big for comprehension. Winning the lottery—that I could imagine—but this . . . not in a million years could I ever have come up with this one.

He was Jesus—Y'shua Mashiach, Alpha and Omega, the Christ, the Lamb of God, Anointed One, Emmanuel, King of Kings, Lord of Lords—and I was going to play Him in a movie.

PART TWO

WALKING

IN HIS JOY

In the
FOOTSTEPS
of JESUS

THE ADVENTURE BEGINS

CHAPTER THREE

"All I could think to do was pray."

*I*T WAS A TWO-DAY JOURNEY to my final destination of Quarzazate, Morocco. Along the way I spent a night in Zurich and a day in Casablanca, and for someone who'd never been in a non-English-speaking country, those were adventures enough in and of themselves. Thank the Lord, He was alongside, taking perfect care of me. Let me share some stories . . .

When word gets out that a guy is going on a trip like mine, everybody and his brother has advice: "Yes, I had a cousin who went to Morocco, and you know what happened to him . . ." "Make sure you watch out for . . ." Fact or fiction, it was enough to make me run down to a bookstore and flip through a travel guide before taking off.

I was thrilled to discover the weather didn't get seriously cold there (boy, was I in for a surprise), but a couple of other things got me worrying. This little book said the government was antagonistic toward anything Christian, and chances were good that Bibles and the like would be confiscated upon entry. It also said in the late 1960s and early '70s an influx of "hippies" had poured into the country and caused problems, so they were suspect of anyone with that kind of appearance—namely long hair and a beard!

So there I was, approaching customs in Casablanca, the only person in line who couldn't speak the language, with a beard, long hair, a suitcase full of Christian books, and a Bible. I'm telling you, with every step closer to this grim-faced agent, my heart pounded harder and harder, and my prayers went up faster and faster. "Lord, get me past this guy. Dear God, don't let him search my bags; keep me from saying something stupid. Come on, Lord, do a miracle!"

Suddenly the agent was right in front of me. I smiled as big as I could. He didn't even look at me. He said something in a language that may as well have been Martian, and I responded, "English. I only speak English." Wrong thing to say—he looked at me as if I had no right to be on his planet. We weren't off to a very promising start, but then a miracle happened. He was thumbing through my passport and asked why I was in the country. I started to tell him as best I could, and the moment he heard the word "actor" his face lit up like the night sky on the Fourth of July: "Actor! Cinema?"

"Yes, cinema . . ." That was all he needed to hear. He got so excited I thought he was going to climb across the desk and give me a kiss. "Cinema! Cinema!" Suddenly he was my best friend in the world, stamping everything he could stamp and waving me through without even checking my pockets. He probably would have given me his firstborn son if I'd asked.

Late that night in the same airport, I was rushing through the terminal to catch my connecting flight to Quarzazate. When I arrived at the gate, I was shocked to find absolutely no one there—no airline personnel, no passengers, no one loitering in the hall. There wasn't even an airplane docked outside the window.

Did they give me the wrong gate? Maybe I'm in the wrong terminal. How can anyone not be here? Could I have missed the flight?

There was a sign next to the gate number, but the message was written in Arabic and French. The clock was ticking and panic was rising fast—this place was so foreign and confusing that the thought of getting stuck there overnight was just about scaring the beard off me. Not having the slightest idea where to turn, I sank into one of those plastic airport chairs and started to seriously pray.

I'm telling you, it was praying like I've never prayed, and this was my specific plea: "Lord, send me somebody—*anybody!*" Suddenly, from down the hall shuffled an elderly Moroccan couple decked from head to toe in traditional jalaba dress. I had never seen anything like these two except in the pages of *National Geographic*. The woman had these exotic henna designs stenciled all over her face, and the old man's feet—wow! I stared, wondering how many times he'd crossed the Sahara with them.

Believe it or not, with all the empty chairs around, the old man plopped himself right next to me, elbow to elbow. He didn't even toss me a glance; he just sat down as if I were invisible. His wife, on the other hand, gave me a huge, toothless smile. I can still see it in my memory to this day. It's hard to explain, but in my utter lack of worldliness, sitting next to these two was like sitting on another planet.

My mind raced all the more. *How can I talk to this guy? Dear God, give me the words to say. What if he hates Americans? What's that stuff all over his wife's face?*

Out of desperation I mustered all my courage, turned toward the old man, and squeezed out, "Quarzazate?" He looked at me with eyes as deep as an ocean and smiled as big as the sky. "Quarzazate," he calmly responded, completely assuring me in every way. With a sigh of thanksgiving, I smiled back into his wise and weathered countenance, finally relaxing in the company of newfound friends.

The Lord had done it—He'd sent the somebody I begged Him for. And you know something? As scary as that old man was to me at first sight, that's how comforting he became in the moment we exchanged smiles. He meant so much to me that night, I often think of him to this day—he and his wife with the henna on her face. I wonder where they are, what they're doing, and if by some remarkable twist of fate we'll ever get the chance to sit together again. As the Moroccans say, "*In challah*"—if God wills it.

Soon I found myself buckled into an AirMaroc four-prop plane that would take me on the final leg of my journey. Staring out the window into the black African night, I tried to imagine what the world below me looked like. There were only seven or eight other passengers on board, all Moroccans. They all appeared to be going home, and I remember being fascinated by that, thinking to myself, *People actually live in a place called Quarzazate.*

There was a little sign in Arabic on the back of the seat in front of me. It was a sight I never imagined I'd see, and I just stared, amazed that I was staring at it. I smiled at the flight attendant; she didn't smile back. I would have loved a cup of coffee but couldn't figure out how to ask for one. There was no moon outside the window that I recall—just black night peppered with stars. I silently tried to put it all together: Two days ago I was picking fleas off my dog in Los Angeles; the night before, touching down in the heart of Zurich; this afternoon, strolling the streets of Casablanca; and now, flying over north Africa, bound for some remote place whose name I couldn't pronounce. Who would have believed it?

My life had been dramatically transformed in a single moment of stepping through an airport metal detector thousands of miles on the other side of the planet. Everything even remotely familiar was gone, and not just gone, but as if it never existed. I'd never felt so completely alone and so utterly dependent on God in my life. So I prayed. I prayed and prayed. It was all I could think to do.

After what felt like forever, the plane turned downward. There was a small huddle of lights below—Quarzazate. My heart leaped a few hundred rpm's, and so did my praying. The landing gear dropped, the lights got closer, and my heart pounded faster. The plane tilted and angled. There was no turning back now—I was in it, and it was real. "Lord, don't let me down; You've gotten me this far. Dear God, be with me now . . ."

As if in a dream, I walked across an asphalt tarmac toward a tiny, cinderblock building. "Please, Lord, don't be going anywhere on me . . ." Following the locals like a puppy, I felt an icy wind blast through my Levi's jacket. "I love You, Jesus. You hear me? I love You."

Through a dirty window, I glimpsed something wonderfully familiar: the smile of Regardt van den Bergh. He was standing at the end of a hallway dressed in sweatpants and a trench coat, jumping up and down like a kid, flanked by a huddle of anxiously staring strangers. "Praise God!"

Out of nowhere—whoosh—a woman grabbed my luggage. "Bruce? Bruce Marchiano? My name is Ihssane, the production coordinator. Follow me, please." Before I could even react, she'd taken my hand and was pulling me past everyone, whisking me through a pair of security guards, shouting something in Arabic over her shoulder.

This woman was so remarkably in command—I remember feeling the physical strength with which she squeezed my hand and sensing for the first time in two days, *Everything is going to be okay.*

A pair of arms suddenly enveloped my shoulders—Regardt. He was a man I'd known only a handful of hours two months before, yet he embraced me like his dearest friend in the world. Handshakes came at me from all around him—F.C., Diana, Hassan, Moody—their names whipped by me like a subway train. Nervous laughter ricocheted off the walls, accented by the crack of a hearty backslap. "It's good to see you, brother!" Regardt was beaming at me.

The next thing I knew, I was in the backseat of a blue Renault, speeding down desert roads, winter roaring through the open windows. The car yanked to a halt, doors bolted wide, my luggage disappeared, and I found myself plopped on a sofa in a hotel lobby, toasting with Moroccan tea and belly-laughing in celebration with people I had met only minutes before.

Regardt was like a schoolboy, "'Jesus' is here! 'Jesus' is here!" The lobby exploded with a traditional Moroccan welcome of music and dance. We drank tea and more tea, we laughed and laughed, and it was all whirling about me so incredibly fast. I was living it, yet all the while watching myself live it, and screaming inside, *Can you believe what's going on, Bruce? You're sitting on a sofa in Africa! They're dancing and singing for you! You're drinking Moroccan tea, for crying out loud!*

After a final round of hugs and handshakes, a door closed behind me and I stood alone again, facing the suite that would be my first Moroccan home. Sudden silence screamed as loudly as the festivities just left behind. A sitting room lay to my left, a hallway in front, and a staircase peeked from the right-hand corner. I chose the stairs.

In the quiet I unpacked, showered, crawled into bed, and read my Bible. Then I pulled out a homemade cassette tape that friends in L.A. had given me and slipped it into my Walkman. I pushed the play button, flipped off the lamp, and lay down in the darkness. It began with a reading of Psalm 95 (NKJV):

Oh come, let us sing to the Lord!
Let us shout joyfully to the Rock of our salvation.
Let us come before His presence with thanksgiving;
Let us shout joyfully to Him with psalms.
For the Lord is the great God, and the great King above all gods.
In His hand are the deep places of the earth;
The heights of the hills are His also.
The sea is His, for He made it;
And His hands formed the dry land.
Oh come, let us worship and bow down;
Let us kneel before the Lord our Maker.
For He is our God,
And we are the people of His pasture,
And the sheep of His hand.

Then came singing. "Come, let us worship and bow down; let us kneel before the Lord our God, our Maker. For He is our God, and we are the people of His pasture." They had gotten together with a piano and recorded worship to the Lord—a sweet taste of the home fellowship that had been a singular oasis to me through the past year and a half of life-desert.

I joined with them, singing into the darkness from my Moroccan bed, "And the sheep of His hand. Yes, the sheep of His hand." That's when it all hit me—the travel, the terror, the uncertainty, the exhaustion, the adventure, the aloneness, the excitement, the unworthiness, the love of friends, and the astounding goodness of God, who had taken my hand in the darkest pit of my life and miraculously led me to this little bedroom on the other side of the world. It was far more than I could handle, and I broke, weeping under the blankets like a baby. "Thank You, Jesus; thank You. I love You so much. Dear God, I love You so much."

That was the last thing I remember. I awoke at 4:00 the next afternoon—16 hours later—with headphones still attached to my ears and the Walkman lying on the pillow.

In the days to come I would meet some of my best friends in the world, battle the devil in the desert, preach the gospel in a first-century marketplace, embrace the blind, dance with children, hear the heartbeat of God like I had never thought possible, and hang from a wooden cross on a hilltop overlooking a thousand-year-old village.

But as I rolled out of bed and fell to my knees, completely unaware that it wasn't morning but afternoon, as I opened the shutters for my first glimpse of Quarzazate in the daylight, I had not the slightest idea of those things that lay ahead. All I could think to do was pray.

QUARZAZATE

CHAPTER FOUR

"They're gathering at the cross."

$\mathcal{I}$N CAPPING OFF THE LAST PAGE OR TWO, a flood of wonderful *Quarzazate* stories lit my imagination, and I just couldn't allow them to fall by the wayside. Hopefully they will strike blessing in your heart.

That's a lesson the Lord has brought to me in the last couple of years—you never know where a blessing in life might drop from, or where a little thing you do that may seem tiny on the surface might be used by the Lord in a big way. Let me quickly tell a story that has nothing to do with Quarzazate but illustrates the point.

In October 1994, I was deep in the South African countryside, driving with my ministry coordinator, Ingrid, toward Johannesburg—four hours to Jan Smuts Airport—to catch a flight.

We were making good time when suddenly I heard a sound coming from my wheel that no one ever wants to hear, especially when winding through the mountains of rural South Africa—*thump-thump-thump-thump*. It was loud and ugly, but foolishly I ignored it and kept driving, even passing two different turnouts. The thump was as stubborn as me, though, and miles later I begrudgingly pulled over for a look.

Getting out of the car, I noticed a huddle of squatters' shacks just below the highway. *Uh-oh.* Forgive me, but my immediate thought was to climb back into the car. You have to understand, the political climate of the area was highly charged and unpredictable, so my concern was more prudence than paranoia. But the wheel couldn't be ignored. The steel belt was hanging on the tire by a thread—a tire that was brand new! Faces began peeking from doorways below, and as I jacked the car up, a lone, male figure stepped out and strode toward me.

Both Ingrid and I began to pray for the Lord's protection. Suddenly he was towering above me. But to my great relief, he was smiling and rattling merrily in a foreign tongue. He didn't speak English but just kept rambling and oddly rubbing his hands together. Ingrid stepped in and they shared a few common words, then he turned and hurried back toward his mud home.

I will never forget the look on Ingrid's face as she told me what he was saying, and why he'd gone back. She was so touched, so humbled. She was smiling and her eyes were misting: "Ach, shame (that's a South African expression)," she said. "Bruce, *he's gone to get you something to clean your hands.*"

The next thing I knew, he was setting a tub of water, a brand-new bar of soap, and a rag in front of me. I nearly burst into tears. It was as moving a thing as I'd ever seen, and not just because it was a display of such goodness, but a display of such *giving.*

You see, the value of that soap to this man was beyond what you or I can understand. It was likely the only one he had or would have for months, and probably something he brought out only on special occasions, like your best china or silverware.

That's hard for our first-world minds to grasp, but having spent most of the last few years in Africa, believe me, I'm more than likely understating this than overstating it. I once went to dinner in one of these homes, and in front of my eyes, proudly displayed alongside the family's most treasured possessions, was a bar of Camay soap. Welcome to the real world.

So here was this fellow, not just being nice, but actually giving of his best. Not once did he ask for a cent or anything in return, he just wanted to bless me.

I don't know who this little girl is, but her picture has been in more magazines across the world than she could imagine. Unfortunately, this sequence is not in the film. We were waiting for a rainstorm to pass, and I just started playing with the children. Set photographer Robby Botha seized the opportunity... "for the kingdom of heaven belongs to such as these."

Two blind men receive their sight on the Jericho Road. These two guys really were blind. Regardt saw them on the street in Quarzazate and hired them. The one in the background is an older man. The one Jesus is touching took care of him, though 90 percent blind himself. Shockingly, the older man spoke great English, and we didn't have to dub him as he spoke, "Lord, we want our sight."

If there's one thing I'm proud of, it's that I'm the first Jesus in film history whose hair moved when the wind blew. On the set at the feeding of the five thousand, notice the sweat glistening and the weathered face—reality. As you can see, I'm having the time of my life, in the footsteps of Jesus.

"I have compassion for these people; they have already been with me three days and have nothing to eat." ..."Where could we get enough bread...to feed such a crowd?" Notice it's Judas whom Jesus is with. Another Regardt touch, including Judas in everything as he undoubtedly would have been included. Notice Jesus' arm around his shoulder. This scene was shot in South Africa long before their first democratic elections of '94. Look at the racial mix. A call for volunteers went out to all Cape Town, and so many showed up (3000-plus) we had to turn people away in spite of the 100° temperature. All cultures and walks of life coming together in Jesus. It was glorious!

"The Man." As much as I discovered Jesus' joy and affection, that's how much I discovered that you don't want to mess with Him either. Here He lets a Pharisee (left foreground) have it with a single look.

Rehearsing the calling of Matthew with apostle Andrew, complete with sunglasses, watching Regardt's technique. We would work a scene improvisationally like this and let it take its own shape, hopefully with the Holy Spirit in control. Regardt assumes the camera position.

Matthew was a despised embezzler and traitor to his people. With everyone expecting Jesus to say, "Woe to you!" He says, "Follow me." What a shocker it must have been. Location: Volibulus, a Roman city erected in North Africa 2000 years ago.

"Taking the five loaves and the two fish and looking up to heaven, he gave thanks...." I must tell you, I was not acting, but truly giving thanks for the wonders I was experiencing.

I remember thinking that the key to playing Jesus was simply to love every single person as if they were the only person on the planet—eye-to-eye, one-on-one, hands-on, intimate. This photo was made into a huge poster and hung in the World Trade Center in Johannesburg, South Africa, for a short while. I am told people flocked to it and stood beneath it, some with silent tears rolling down their cheeks.

"The teachers of the law and the Pharisees sit in Moses' seat. So you must obey them and do everything they tell you. But do not do what they do, for they do not practice what they preach." The line is drawn, and the march toward Golgotha begins. Notice the faces of John and Peter to the right and the extras to my left. Though in the background, they were really getting into it. You could cut the tension on the set that day with a dull knife.

Gentle...lowly...riding on a donkey. Jesus' idea of being a king. I remember sensing the irony—in no time these same people would be shouting. "Crucify him!" and Jesus was the only one who knew it. The Moroccan donkey's name was Rocky. Regardt recalls seeing the way I was sitting astride the donkey, as opposed to the traditional image of Him sitting sidesaddle, and the realization hit him: "What we're doing here is very different."

As I washed the grease away, I looked at his clothes, his house, his ribs poking through his skin—this man who'd done me such a kindness. I wanted to thank him somehow, so I reached into my wallet and gave him a 20-rand note.

Now before you think I'm some wonderful philanthropist, please understand that 20 rand is less than five U.S. dollars. Believe me, it was no big sacrifice. But to this man—Philemon was his name—this was a *very big deal.* When he saw that 20-rand note, he went absolutely ballistic, exploding in tears, leaping and jumping in excitement. He danced and whirled and hollered and fell to his knees in a display of emotion the likes of which I've never witnessed before or since. His heart was literally pulsating through the thin skin of his chest as he threw his arms up and screamed to the sky, tears cascading down his ebony face.

I couldn't understand a word he was yelling—except one. It was a word he kept shouting again and again, and every time I heard it I couldn't believe my ears. The word was *"Jesu,"* and I don't think I need to explain what *Jesu* means.

This man who had so blessed me, this man I thought was going to harm me, this man who was dancing circles around me—*this man was a brother in the Lord.* And watching him who had nothing scream such thanksgiving to his Savior for a mere five bucks remains one of the most awe-inspiring experiences of my life.

Philemon took us to meet his wife. Visitors were not a typical sight, and her eyes flashed with confusion. But that quickly turned to open-mouthed disbelief as her husband's hysteria sank in. He was breathlessly waving the note as evidence, and all she could do was stare, blank-faced.

I took her hand and slipped a second note between her fingers. Oh, my goodness—I should have checked with her physician first because she literally stopped breathing. Her eyes froze and her face dropped limp with emotional overload. Silent tears began to drip from her eyes and tumble down her quivering cheeks. Philemon's eyes burst afresh as well, and he danced all the more.

It went on and on like that. None of us wanted it to stop. We could have stayed the entire day, but there was a plane to catch. After meeting their five kids and other villagers, we joined hands and prayed together as one. Philemon and I embraced in a final hug—brothers—then it was back on the road toward Johannesburg.

I don't think Ingrid and I spoke a word in the car for a good hour. What could either of us say? On the surface, a chance meeting—a flat tire, dirty hands, a family in need of a few bucks. But, no—that was a new tire, and it's not like me to drive past two turnouts like that.

Mist began to fall, then rain. I reached to flip on the windshield wipers. My hands—they were so clean. I couldn't help but wonder what they would have looked like if not for my brother Philemon. *Jesu! Jesu!* He'd danced himself into exhaustion, and it was as poignant a life experience as I've ever had.

The locals told me Quarzazate means "place of silence," and it is a place so remarkably dear to me, daily I beg the Lord to take me back there. First, the town and its residents just stole my heart away, these people who drew their water from a well and rode donkey carts to the marketplace. Their innocence and utter contentment were breathtaking. Add to that the sense of stepping back in time a thousand years—it was all so completely disarming.

But the real root of my love affair with Quarzazate is in what was birthed there—my walk in the footsteps of Jesus, as well as lifelong

brotherhoods and friendships. It was a time of such humble innocence and trembling before God. It was a time of timidly "stepping
out of the boat" and being scooped up by the Lord again and again.
It was a time of peeking into His mighty heart and being absolutely
astounded. It was a time when a handful of ordinary guys, complete
and utter fools in the eyes of the world, drew together and clung to
each other, confident only in that we were called by God, but without
the slightest assurance that anything would actually work.

Imagine, if you will, a handful of grown men huddled in a Moroccan
hotel room at 5:30 A.M., begging the Lord through glassy eyes to do
what only He could do. An actor, a film director, a cinematographer,
a production designer—skilled professionals praying like little boys:
deeply humbled, desperately dependent, and without any idea of what
we'd gotten ourselves into. Of such are my memories of Quarzazate.

Let me tell you a fun story about these men and a Moroccan tradi-
tion called the *hammam* (or as we Westerners irreverently refer to it,
the steam bath). The Moroccans have made an art out of their hammam. They go there to cleanse, massage, and purify their bodies. But
to a couple of South Africans and an unsophisticated American, it
was just a place to steam away the winter chill, sweat out the aches of
a long day, and pray for the work that was being accomplished.

I'll never forget my first trip to the hammam. Regardt, F.C. Hamman,
our Moroccan cinematographer, and I went together. The three of us
strolled into the dressing room (or should I say, *un*dressing room),
laughing and joking, excited to shed our clothes and climb into that
nice, hot hammam after a day of scouting third-world locations.
There was one slight problem, though: Sitting behind a desk directly
facing us was a *female* hammam attendant, casually knitting a baby
sweater. She had one eye on her needlework and the other on us.
There was no door to close, no curtain to draw, no wall to separate us.
As the saying goes, there was "nowhere to run, nowhere to hide." F.C.
asked if there was a changing room somewhere, but she spoke no
English and couldn't figure out what he was saying. So there we were
stuck—three grown men sitting on a little wooden bench, staring at
this woman, feeling (and probably looking) like three schoolboys.

Of course we could have turned around and walked out, but it
seemed like such a cop-out. How could we let a woman with a pair

of knitting needles back us down like that? Thoroughly embarrassed, we just sat there for the longest time, each hoping the other would take that inevitable first step.

Then one of us came up with a plan: We would slowly take off our shoes and socks, giving her a subtle hint. She would pick up on it and slip out the door. So doing our best to appear cool, we each began untying first one lace, then the other; one shoe—long pause—then the other; one sock—long pause—then the other.

We must have worked at it for a good five minutes, but still she didn't budge. Someone then suggested that peeling off a shirt would surely do the trick. We gave it a try, but again to no avail. Our little knitter was going nowhere. Of course, this was her job—to attend the hammam—and if she'd seen one man undress, she'd seen a million. It really was no big deal to her, but to us it was madness!

Finally, after probably 20 minutes, we just decided to buck up and dive in. We cleared our throats, lowered our voices, and began ripping away at buttons and zippers. You never saw three men get undressed faster in your life. I remember tripping over my pant leg and falling, I was rushing so wildly. Not one of us dared a glance to see if she was looking—we didn't want to know—we just raced by her, leaving our clothes in a trail behind. No doubt the Lord was thoroughly entertained, watching His kids bungle around, held at bay by a woman with two knitting needles.

Believe it or not, we became regulars in the hammam. Regardt, F.C., and I met there most every night, occasionally joined by others. It became our prayer room at the end of each day—three worn-out men, sweat rolling down their limbs, lifting high praises to the living God, thanking Him for the day's victories and begging Him for tomorrow's, pleading for His mercies to fall on these lovely Moroccan people. It was glorious.

When I think back on Quarzazate, I think about the hammam—and I smile. Sometimes (like now) I get a little misty-eyed; sometimes, real quiet, but I always smile. Ah, sweet Quarzazate—the word has become a special greeting between Regardt, Bruce Rudnick, and me: "Quarzazate, my 'Bru'!" It calls to mind an era of astounding purpose and the coming together at one time and place of everything our lives were about: filmmaking, Jesus, exotic locations, adventure.

We were a band of clumsy brothers in the Lord, knit together in all-out dedication to the call on our lives. Shielded by distance from "the suits" and yielded in awe to Jehovah, it was the closest thing to heaven any of us had ever tasted—Quarzazate.

Here's a quote from my first journal entry of the film shoot:

> I don't know what day it is, except to say I arrived in Quarzazate on Saturday, and am guessing today is Thursday. We've just completed our second day of shooting—yesterday the temptations in the wilderness, today some preaching in Galilee as well as minor confrontations with Pharisees.
>
> The Lord is with me and the entire production every step of the way. All are not just working hard, but high-spirited. Even the non-Christians are working with a sense of doing something important. Hundreds—crew, extras, bystanders, police—are sitting around listening to the Word of God all day, and it is glorious.

Seeing those words sparks in my heart the memory of our first day of filming: Jesus in the wilderness. The entire cast and crew assembled in the hotel lobby as the Moroccan sun peeked over the Atlas Mountains. Regardt stood in the center of us all and launched the shoot by boldly announcing his complete and total allegiance to the lordship of Jesus Christ. Then he led us in a prayer of submission, dedication, consecration, and servanthood. What a way to begin!

The next thing I knew, we were all in cars speeding toward the desert outskirts. You can't imagine how pumped I was, as was the entire team. For just about everyone there, months of preparation were boiling down to a single moment, and though it all looked good on paper, none of us knew for sure if anything was going to work. We would find out very quickly, though. In less than an hour Regardt would yell, "Action!" Then it would be like a runaway train. I can't tell you the excitement!

My first challenge reared its head immediately. The way Regardt and I saw these wilderness scenes, Jesus would be walking barefoot, but a quick examination of the desert floor showed a blanket of jagged rocks and needle-sharp thorns. We discussed options, and though it certainly wouldn't be fun, we decided to go for it anyway. The aches and pains of actually walking through the thorns would lend an authenticity to the scene that I could never approach on even my best acting day, and both Regardt and I wanted it.

So the sandals came off, Regardt called his first "Action!" and I moved out. It took all of two seconds to learn that I was going to get much more than I bargained for. With every step I landed on one barbed thing or another, sending flashes of sharp pain through the soles of my city-boy feet.

It may seem nuts, but you must understand, I wanted it to look not just good, but *great,* and the best way to ensure that was for me to actually "do" it, as opposed to pretend it.

"Take two!"

"Take three!"

"Take four!"

Regardt would yell "Cut!" and I'd either freeze where I stood or collapse onto a rock if there was one close enough. Then the makeup and wardrobe attendants would literally rush to my aid.

That sequence played itself out over and over, all day long. I'll never forget looking down at Khadija, our Moroccan makeup assistant, as she held my feet in her lap, tweezing out thorns, cleaning cuts, and massaging bruises. She did that take after take. Then there was Amina, our wardrobe assistant, rushing me my sandals and gently slipping them onto my feet for the short walk back to first position. Those women were beyond angels that day.

But as if the thorns and rocks weren't enough, Regardt then led me to the crest of a steep incline and explained the action for another shot—an exhausted Jesus would crawl up the incline with everything He's got, then, just before making it over the ridge, slip and tumble back down for His first encounter with the devil.

"Thanks for the inspired scene, Reg" (I gave up trying to pronounce his name and started calling him "Reg"). This was no simple task. Looking down the hill, all I could see were boulders. Some were the size of watermelons and some the size of me, but every one looked just the right size to inflict serious damage on a human body.

The shot would require a stunt that in a typical Hollywood production would consume the better part of a morning just to plan, coordinate, rehearse, and secure. A veteran stuntman would take serious precautions and pad himself from head to toe before even a walk-through. As for me, I'd only done one previous stunt in my entire career, and that was a cakewalk compared to this monster!

But I'll tell you something—as I stood staring at the dangers below, I felt an overwhelming sense of divine protection, and as clear as day the words rose in my heart, "You won't get hurt. You'll get a little banged up, but you won't get hurt." Think I'm crazy if you will, but I can remember it like yesterday—those exact words indescribably forming in my heart.

We didn't rehearse the scene even once, except for a walk-through for the camera. I tumbled down that hill for five, six, maybe even seven takes. The crew was absolutely astonished. Our first assistant director, Diana, on the other hand, was in a rage. She exploded at Regardt for allowing me to do such a thing, and you know what? She was absolutely right. It was foolish for me to do the stunt even once, let alone take after take, unprotected and uncoordinated. If I broke an arm or leg or even blackened an eye, the entire production would be forced to shut down.

59

But you see, the Lord wasn't going to let anything like that happen. I knew it, Regardt knew it, and we moved with an against-all-odds, against-all-reason, against-all-human-wisdom sense of complete confidence. We knew without a single doubt that God was going before us, and He wouldn't allow failure of any kind. We were so focused on that, it never crossed our minds that there was any real danger in anything we attempted. We felt completely shielded, as if we were encased in some sort of holy insulation. Again, that may sound crazy, but it was an overwhelming sense.

When I bathed that evening, I checked everything from the bottoms of my feet to the top of my head. What I saw was exactly what I knew I'd see: an occasional cut, scrape, or bruise. My feet were pretty tender, but no real wounds, no broken bones. My body stood at the end of that day exactly as I'd been told it would stand: *a little banged up, but not hurt.* God's faithfulness was astounding.

Journal: February 2

Ministry is happening all around us. The nonbelieving crew is asking questions left and right. There are so many individual stories happening all around us—I'm so tired I've not been able to sit and write them here in detail. This is exhausting work. After just a couple scenes today, I'm beat. There's no way a person could keep this pace of concentration and emotional expense—it's wearing. But the Lord will carry me! Praise God. Yesterday Regardt was giving me direction, and I zoned on him. As I looked in his face all I could think was, *I will never not know this man.*

One of my dearest Quarzazate memories involves Regardt (no surprise there). Forgive me if this embarrasses you, Reg, but I've just got to tell this story.

One fundamental member of any production crew is the clapper-loader. He's the guy responsible for loading and unloading the film magazine. I can't overstate his responsibility. If he accidentally exposes the footage, it could mean tens, maybe even hundreds of thousands of dollars down the drain; and he would not only be fired, but as they say in Hollywood, "You'll never work in this town again."

In 12 years in the industry, not only have I never seen film get exposed, but I've never even heard of it. That's how terrible a mistake it is—it simply never happens. Well, you guessed it—on the set of *Matthew,* with a schedule that allowed no margin for error, it happened. We'd just finished a Jesus/apostles en route scene, and just in the nick of time because the sun was sinking fast behind the palm trees. It had been another long, hard day in a succession of long, hard days. Everyone was looking forward to hearing, "That's a wrap!" but what we heard instead was the sound of a grown man weeping.

The entire set froze, and all eyes turned to see the clapper-loader buckled on his knees in the dirt with a film magazine lying in front of him. He was sobbing like a baby. No one knew what was going on, so Bernard, the camera focus-puller, cautiously walked over and bent down to him. Words were whispered, and Bernard's face went white— the film had been exposed, and much of the day's work destroyed.

Murmurs began to rip through cast and crew like fire through dry grass. The clapper-loader just knelt in the dirt, blubbering over and over, "Why on *this* film?" Bernard, a gentle man, softly said with a pat on the back, "Get yourself together," and went to deliver the grim news to Regardt. With his every step, we all braced for what would certainly be an unleashing of director's rage.

I will never forget Reg's face dropping at Bernard's whispered words. A hushed, "He what?" leaked from his lips, followed by a silence we could have driven a convoy through. Then he turned toward everyone and quietly said, "Everyone makes mistakes. Some are little ones, and some are big ones." The next thing we saw was Regardt and F.C. crouched over that broken clapper-loader, comforting him like a son. It blew the clapper-loader's mind; it blew my mind; it blew everyone's mind. I can put it no better than my journal:

> No one did so much as raise a finger to him—instead, Regardt and F.C. ministered to the guy, who was devastated. All eyes were watching, and all saw the Christian in Regardt in the way he handled it. It was testimony to the goodness in his heart. As a result, many questions are being asked today about Jesus—they all know. Praise God. His work is being done.

All the proselytizing in the world could never approach an act of godly compassion such as that silently spoken into every heart that laid eyes on it.

Another Regardt story: One morning Reg came to me and said, "Bruce, the Lord showed me that through us He would create 'rivers in the desert,' here in Quarzazate." I smiled but thought to myself, *That's cute, Reg, but I think you're reaching this time. There's nothing but dry, cracked ground on every level out here.*

This was one serious desert we were in, physically and spiritually. As lovely as the people were, they were poor and tired, and their spirits were crushed and oppressed. It may have been a "place of silence," but it was not a place of joy. And physically, the land hadn't seen rain for more than a year, and the people were in the throes of a drought. Every day, driving back to the hotel, we'd cross a bridge over a river bed that had been dry so long it was identifiable as such only because the bridge hung over it.

Well, to use the lead-in again, "You guessed it." One day we looked to the sky and saw storm clouds moving in. None of us could believe our eyes. Within hours it was raining; and it didn't just rain that day, it rained the next day, and the next, and the next. We were forced to shut down and film what we could between showers.

I remember shooting Simon the Leper's Bethany feast during that time. We were in a magnificently ornate room in the middle of a centuries-old Casbah. It rained so seldom in the region, the king who'd built this room didn't bother to put a roof over it. Consequently, just as the woman was anointing "Jesus" with her costly perfume, the Lord in His infinite sense of humor decided to anoint us all with some perfume of His own in the form of an in-house shower! It gave everyone a good laugh at the time, but the clock was ticking away on our shooting schedule, and the rain was putting a dent in our plans. Little did anyone know, the Lord had other plans—plans far superior and far more important than ours.

You see, the Moroccans needed the rain desperately. While we were worrying about our schedule, their land was being abundantly restored. And coming out of nowhere like it did, the people of Quarzazate believed it was a miracle from God. They further believed it was our feet (Christian feet) on their soil that brought them this miracle.

A day or two after that first rain fell, we were driving back to the hotel when I looked out the window to see the Atlas Mountains through scattered clouds—they were blanketed in snowpack. And as we turned to cross that now-familiar bridge, I saw an even more impossible sight: a steady stream of crystalline, life-giving water snaking from those mountains and stretching through that riverbed as far as the eye could follow. In spite of the icy temperatures, the locals and their children were lining that stream, filling jug after jug, splashing and playing as if it were summer. Silently my lips moved, fogging the car window with Regardt's words of just days before, "rivers in the desert."

The Lord had done it, and I had to believe the physical reality confronting my eyes was representative of the more significant work He was doing in Moroccan lives. I had to believe that as the Word was being poured out on Quarzazate, rivers of *living* water were coursing through desert hearts He longed to heal and renew. I'll never know for sure till I get to heaven, but sitting here today I have no doubt about that whatsoever.

Here's another Quarzazate story: the story of the filming of Jesus on the Jericho Road to Jerusalem.

Reg planned to film the scene simply. We were on location in a tiny Berber village on the outskirts of Quarzazate. It was ancient, complete with crumbling mud walls lining pathways that had no doubt been walked for centuries.

On the edge of this village was a huge pit, unusually and magnificently lush with vegetation. Wild olive and palm trees stood proudly, creating the shadiest spot any of us had seen in Morocco thus far. It was so pretty, in fact, Regardt decided to have Jesus and His disciples walk through this sun-dappled grove and up a dirt path toward camera, where He would stop to heal two blind men.

It's a lovely scene in the film, as one of these blind fellows opens his eyes for the first time in life only to look straight into the face of His smiling Savior. Can you imagine? He stretches his bent, dirty hands to hold and caress this divine sight, making certain it isn't a dream. Jesus responds with a display of love so astounding it almost outshines the healing itself. He takes those filthy beggar hands in His own and *kisses* them. I'm telling you, His love is so far beyond what any one of us can imagine!

For obvious reasons we were all excited to shoot what would undoubtedly be one of the most tender scenes in the film. The camera and crew ready, Jesus and the Twelve marched into the grove and confidently took positions, eagerly awaiting Regardt's "Action!"

But there was an odd sort of problem. The villagers playing the crowd of followers refused to come down into the pit with us. No one knew why, but the whole lot of them mutinied; they just stood giggling and shaking their heads as if to say, "No way." Looking around, we noticed it wasn't just the extras who were giggling, but all the onlooking villagers as well. Some were actually doubled over in open laughter. Exactly why, no one had any idea. Finally, with some coaxing from Moody, our Moroccan assistant director, the extras reluctantly plodded down the path and took positions around us. That made the villagers explode in hysterics all the more.

Meanwhile, those of us in the pit became increasingly aware of a rather unpleasant odor wafting through the air. It seemed to be coming from everywhere, and the more we smelled it, the more disgustingly familiar it became; and the more familiar it became, the more closely we examined the premises. What our eyes eventually discovered confirmed the very horror our noses were beginning to suspect. It was a shocking reality to be sure, but it was reality nonetheless: This lovely grove we were camped in was nothing other than the village toilet—and from the looks of it, it had been the village toilet for centuries. I'll tell you, if ever "Jesus" had a trial, this certainly was it.

So what did we do? We shot everything as planned. The camera was down, the scene was established, and the clock was ticking; so we held our breath, tiptoed through the land mines, and went with it—take after take after take. . . .

Boy, did we have some laughs at ourselves over that one.

———————

Then there's my dear brother Bruce Rudnick. I don't know that I've ever met anyone with such all-out love, such burning passion for Jesus. I know for sure I've never met anyone so remarkably without self-consciousness, self-promotion, or personal reserve when it comes to Jesus. The first time I laid eyes on Bruce he was sitting at a banquet table downing a Moroccan feast in the hotel restaurant. He'd just flown into Quarzazate and must have been incredibly hungry because he was eating as fast as his fork could fly. But when he saw my face, he dropped everything and almost leaped across the table. He came at me with a huge bear hug, smiling wildly, teeth full of rice and vegetables, so excited to finally meet the guy who was going to play Jesus.

In a voice that's a cross between sandpaper and a bass fiddle, Bruce talked about how thrilled he was to see me and what a wonderful time we were going to have together. I, on the other hand, was completely taken aback. *Who is this maniac? Somebody get him off me!* Little did I know, this wild-eyed man would quickly become one of my closest friends in the world.

I remember the afternoon we really crossed that line into a vital brotherhood. It was the day before we filmed Golgotha. Cast and crew had the day off, and Bruce and I thought it would be a good idea to go to the location and pray, so we slipped into our walking shoes and began the trek.

Now, in case you've never experienced Africa, let me give you a travel tip: Whenever you ask an African where a place is, he or she will always answer, "It's just there," as if it's around the corner. Be forewarned: "It's just there" could mean anything from around the corner to a three-day journey over two mountain ranges! Our "it's just there" ended up being a hard two-hour walk, winding through a maze of muddy byways and ancient villages. It wasn't exactly luxurious, but it was exciting to be off the beaten track and mixing with the Moroccan villagers.

The sun was beating down following days of rain, and I remember Bruce going into shop after shop in a dry-mouthed quest for something cold to drink. It was hilarious to watch. The shopkeepers tried to sell him everything from shoe polish to chickens, but poor Bruce—there wasn't a Coca-Cola anywhere in sight. And so we walked and walked, and talked and talked. It was good, *real* talk.

"Golgotha" was a breathtaking sight. It rose a mound of barren black rock, ominously peaked with three wooden crosses the art department had already erected. They were visible all over the countryside, and as Bruce and I stood taking them in, I couldn't help but think their presence screamed a silent message of the love of Jesus to every Moroccan who beheld them.

We began to scale the slope. It was no simple task—all loose rock and no definite path to follow. We scrambled up the incline, surprisingly steep at times, stopping every so often to catch our breath and take in the panorama: cultivated fields, rural villages, and desert expanse stretching beyond the horizon. We were literally looking back in time, seeing civilization more or less as it had been seen from this hill for a thousand years.

Finally we came over the crest, and what we saw stopped us in our tracks. Local villagers, young and old. Tens of them, sitting on rocks and in the dirt—sitting beneath the three crosses. Bruce and I were speechless. Every so often one of them would walk over and touch the crosses or just stand looking up at them. Other than that, no one was doing or saying anything—just sitting there and staring. And more villagers were teeming up the slope from all directions.

What this sight spoke to both our hearts was beyond words. We stood for the longest time, almost afraid to breathe. Finally Bruce underscored what lay in front of our eyes in a way only he could. "They're gathering at the cross," he whispered in hushed awe. We stood silent on that one for quite a while as well.

Eventually it was time to pray. We prayed for the success of the next day's work, for the people sitting around us, for the town of Quarzazate, and all of Morocco as well. We prayed for Regardt, and that the cross of Jesus reenacted would bring a flow of real redemption into every heart witnessing it. We prayed and prayed and prayed.

On the long walk back, Bruce, who is Jewish, told me of his heart for his people. He confided that his life's passion was to go to Israel someday and share the good news that their long-awaited Messiah had come, and His name is Y'shua. We walked and talked and laughed the afternoon away, and all the while the Lord quietly wove bonds of brotherhood between us.

The next day I would hang atop that hill for the better part of 12 hours, and my new friend would pray for me the entire time. Suspended from the beam, every joint and muscle screaming for release, I'd lift my head and look over the crowd, and there, behind everyone, would stand Bruce's lone figure, lips moving in whispered intercession. It's a sight I'll never forget as long as I live. *Quarzazate, my "Bru." Quarzazate.*

There are many stories—far too many to recount. Stories of adventure, love, and brotherhood; stories of the wonders of God revealed and tasted. It was a humbling, thrilling time, a time curled up at the feet of the Father, of "Dad," feasting on His fun and faithfulness. It was a time of being comforted, consumed, filled, and fully occupied by the reality of the living God.

As I sat quietly by myself on the airplane that would fly me out of Quarzazate and Morocco—out of this exotic land that had revealed so much of God's goodness toward me—I wrote these words in my journal:

> As we pass over Casablanca en route to our next location in South Africa, I pray the Lord's peace in this place. . . . *In challah,* I will return. The emotional roller coaster of this time has been remarkable. I'm not able now to assess it or even remember it with any due justice. As I look back, I see: a ten-year-old boy, Joelle, petting my foot; the heartbreak as I looked over the crowd in "Korazin"; Sarah's face as she looked at me atop Golgotha; Bruce, and the day spent with him; hammam with "my brus"; flowers brought to my room by giggling chambermaids; a ruffian telling me I'm better than Charles Bronson; Khadija picking thorns from my feet; "Aisau!" (Jesus) from every corner; dancing

with the extras in the Casbah; an anointing with oil; "They're gathering at the cross"; sheeps' heads at the produce market; the blood on my arm; watching the nail go through my hand; *"Eloi Eloi llama sabacthani"*—just to rattle off a few.

God has been so good to me here. So much more to come.

Quarzazate was such a remarkable adventure; as I sit here today my heart aches to live it all again. And so I wrap up this chapter praying over your life the sweetest, most abundant blessing I can think to pray over anyone's life:

Quarzazate to you and yours, friend.
Quarzazate!

JESUS, MAN OF JOY

CHAPTER FIVE

Therefore God, your God, has set you above your companions by anointing you with the oil of joy.

HEBREWS 1:9

*I*F I'VE HEARD THE COMMENT ONCE, I've heard it a million times—and I don't ever want to stop hearing it! It usually goes something like this: "I never knew Jesus was so alive, so passionate, so exciting, so *full of joy!*"

For the very first time, people have been discovering this Savior who joyously loves them. Some of them were confirmed atheists; some of them had been sitting in church pews for decades. I was in a church recently where *Matthew* was shown. Afterward the pastor stood before his congregation, tearfully confessing and asking their forgiveness for years of pharisaical hypocrisy and self-righteousness. Another pastor told me, "I've studied Jesus for nine years of my life, and I learned more about Him tonight than in all those years put together." And I'll never forget an elderly couple pulling next to me in their Mercedes as I stood on a street corner. The window rolled down, and this gentle old fellow said, "My wife and I have been Christians all our lives, but last night we realized we never knew Jesus

71

at all"—*Matthew* had been presented to their rural community the night before. Then there's the 14-year-old girl who approached me in a dimly lit parking lot late one night. She was a satanist—until that afternoon when she discovered true love and new life in Jesus as *Matthew* was presented in her high school.

The stories go on and on. Through *Matthew* I've seen the Lord melt the hardest of hearts into tears of repentance. I've seen the Lord melt stone-cold husbands into men sobbingly embracing their long-neglected wives. I've seen Him crumble walls of anger and prejudice between hate-filled men of different races. I've seen Him bridge canyons of arrogance and self-righteousness between leaders of opposing religious traditions. And it is that simple nuance—joy in the persona of Jesus—that seems to be "key": blessing the people, exciting them, often shocking them, and ultimately drawing them to their knees.

Personally I've received many accolades because of it. I've been called a "creative genius," "a brilliant young actor," a "shoo-in award winner," and even an "instrument of God's self-revelation." Deserved or not, that has all been a sweet blessing, but let me set the record straight. Presenting Jesus as a "Man of Joy" was no creation of mine. It was nothing I came up with either as a believer or an actor; in fact, and this may surprise some, at the time it was something of a revelation to me as well. Here is how it all came to be.

December 8, 1992—the day following my audition with Regardt—the two of us sat together in the L.A. Hilton restaurant to discuss the film. I'd had many meetings with directors in my years as an actor, but I'd never had a meeting with the likes of Regardt van den Bergh. This was a director who directed from his knees. With all the note-paper and actor's stuff in my valise that day, little did I know the only thing I needed was the one thing I'd left at home: a Bible. Regardt, on the other hand, was fully prepared: Tucked into his back pocket was a travel-size New International Version Bible.

Regardt was clearly excited from the outset and eager to get past protocol. We ordered. The waiter took our menus and left two cups of coffee. The very second those formalities were out of the way, with sparks leaping from his eyes, Regardt dropped a hand into his back pocket and whipped that little Bible out with the lightning speed of Wyatt Earp and Billy the Kid combined. I'd never seen anything like it! (Over the next four months I'd see that quick action so many times, I've come to name that Bible of his "Regardt's little six-shooter.")

So there we were in this upscale L.A. restaurant, surrounded by power suits doing power lunches, and this man I'd known only an hour was flying through his well-worn Bible, blazing on about God's faithfulness and directives with all the excitement of a kid on Christmas morning. We sat like that for the next three hours: a director with nothing but a Bible full of promises and an actor with nothing but fright and wonder.

Little did I know, as I sat wondering what I was getting myself into, that the God who hand-carved heaven and earth was cementing us in brotherhood for purposes that would stand beyond anyone's imaginings.

At one point during that lunch, Regardt spoke a handful of words that would become cornerstone to everything we did when the cameras rolled. They were words that would springboard countless transformed lives as already described. With all the confidence of a man who knows the prompting of the Holy Spirit and trusts the Word of God, Regardt leaned over the table, looked me square in the eye, and said:

> Bruce, I have one word for you: *joy.* He was anointed with the oil of joy, and *that's* what set Him apart from everyone else—Hebrews 1:9. Bruce, I believe that's what the Lord wants us to do in *Matthew*—to present Jesus as a *Man of Joy.*

Big words; thunderous, daring, brave new words.

And that's where it all began—that afternoon, over that lunch, spoken by Regardt van den Bergh—a man who made his every decision on his knees alongside a Messianic Jew also named Bruce in a Cape Town production office. *Hebrews 1:9 . . . that's what the Lord wants us to do . . . JOY.*

Confession time: I wish I could tell you I had an immediate witness to those words but the truth is, I don't recall having any reaction to them at all. I was just too overwhelmed in that meeting to do much of anything other than nod and grunt, let alone think. *Jesus joyful*—I'd never given it consideration one way or the other. Generally Jesus seemed to be presented as solemn and serenely detached, and the only place I'd ever seen Him smile was in children's Bibles. None of that went through my mind at the time, but I'll tell you, somehow Regardt's

73

words registered deeply with me because, in the coming weeks, every time I heard the word "joy," my heart perked to attention and Regardt's voice whispered all over again, "I have one word for you. . . ."

And that's exactly what happened. Suddenly every time I turned around it seemed that word would pop up. I know it is a fairly common word, especially in Christian circles. But this was different. Let me explain. When news traveled about my involvement with *Matthew,* my circle of friends rallied around me like champions. They came at me with books, tapes, and even Hallmark cards, but more than anything else, they came with prayer. I can't tell you how many prayer meetings were organized on my behalf, and for some reason for the first time everyone seemed to be praying the exact same thing for me: *joy.* Folks prayed I would know joy, experience it, display it, live it; people prayed it would be stamped in my heart and on my forehead for all the world to see—joy, joy, and more joy. It was crazy! And every time it crossed my ears, it grabbed my attention like a lightning bolt.

Then came a real coup de grace. A friend, Teres, phoned to tell me a story that is so simple but carried a profound message.

Teres is a kind of honorary aunt to three kids she's affectionately given the titles of The Bunny, The Buddy, and The Budley. Don't ask me where the nicknames came from, but The Bunny is a beautiful little girl, eight years old at the time of the story, who *loves* the Lord Jesus. Shortly after my big news became big news, Teres told The Bunny she knew a guy who was going to play Jesus in a movie. What that little girl said in reply was beyond amazing, "Well, I sure hope he *smiles* a lot because Jesus in the other Jesus movies never smiled, and I know that Jesus smiles all the time." What's that line about wisdom from the mouths of babes?

I can't help but recall a Scripture I spoke in front of the camera: "I praise you, Father, Lord of heaven and earth, because you have hidden these things from the wise and learned and revealed them to *little children.*"

Maybe that's why Jesus enjoyed kids so much—not just because they were adorable and His special little creations, but maybe also because they were the only ones who truly understood Him, who truly loved Him just the way He was and allowed Him to love them just the way they were. In any event, The Bunny's wisdom lit fireworks in my heart. I remember hanging up the phone and thinking, *The Lord is trying to tell me something here.* I prayed, "Lord, if this is You, drive the point home; I'm all ears." That's a prayer He didn't waste a second in answering.

But the real clincher came a few weeks later. I'd begun my research into the Gospel, and all was going well but for two things. The first was that the Matthew study guide I was using came in two volumes, and I was only able to find the first. No problem. I figured by the time I'd finished with the first volume, the bookstore would be restocked with volume two.

Second, I needed trustworthy material on the *human* personality of Jesus. But as I asked around, I was shocked to discover no one knew of such a book. Every suggestion I received missed the mark, always focusing instead on His divinity. I can't tell you how frustrated I got about that. How would I be able to present the human Jesus without some kind of specific guide in that regard?

Well, when I had exhausted the first volume of my commentary, I scurried to the bookstore assuming the shelves would be refilled.

Surprise—I failed to consider it was just after Christmas, when retail stocks were depleted and restocking halted for year-end inventories. I tried outlet after outlet, hearing the same thing everywhere: "Sorry, but we're out."

My frustration meter went off the scale. I couldn't afford to lose even one day to searching, and it was bizarre the way everyone seemed to have a stock of volume ones but no volume twos.

Finally I found a store a good ten miles away that had a lone copy. "Hold it for me; I'll be right there!" The store closed in just 30 minutes, so I got fast directions, jumped into my truck, and sped off.

Rain was pouring and every inch of L.A. freeway was bumper-to-bumper. I crawled along in first gear, grumbling all the way: "I don't get it, Lord. I'm just trying to do what You want. Why are You making it so difficult?" Finally, there it was—a tiny Christian bookstore tucked into downtown Glendale. With just moments to spare, I squeezed through the glass doors and rushed to the counter. The guy was closing the cash register, and though he looked all over, he couldn't find my commentary on hold anywhere. That nearly sent me through the roof! He pointed to the commentary section across the room, where two customers stood. I bolted for it with predator intensity—nothing and nobody was going to come between me and my volume two.

As I approached, I could see the cover—*at last, you're mine!* Reaching past a customer, I wrapped a hungry claw around it. As I did so, my knuckles scraped against a small paperback sitting face-front alongside it. The flamboyant cover art was a stark contrast to the scholarly looking covers surrounding. I could tell immediately that, though it was in the commentary section, this book was no commentary—*somehow it had been misplaced there.* The title was big, bright, and impossible to miss. It was a title of four words that stopped me cold in my tracks and made my heart leap out of my chest:

Jesus, Man of Joy

I took it in my hands and just stared. It was one of those moments when everything around freezes and becomes a blur. To a passerby, it was a guy looking at a book, but to that guy, it was a turning point—it was from God. Without even glancing at the table of contents, I bought that little book, and as I silently drove the rain-soaked highway homeward, my heart was pounding as fast as the windshield wipers. God had led me to that book as surely as He'd led me to *Matthew*, and I knew it. He needed me to clearly understand that 2000 years ago Jesus was indeed a Man of Joy, and what He wanted me to do as an actor 2000 years later was portray Him as such.

After rushing home from the bookstore, I dove into it. Every page was loaded with gems, and I couldn't highlight phrases or scribble notes fast enough. By the time I climbed into bed that night I had a treasure trove of key phrases that would carry me through the shoot from Day 1 to Wrap. This little paperback with the colorful title was the guide I'd been hunting for.

That night, focus and research took a turn. As I sought to confirm that joy of Jesus in the Word, it became so blatantly obvious I couldn't believe I'd never caught it before. Suddenly it was everywhere, screaming from the pages of Scripture: joy!

Jesus began jumping off the page at me as well—His realness and strength, the sparkle in His eyes, the spring in His gait, the heartiness in His laugh, the genuineness of His touch; His passion, playfulness, excitement, and vitality: His *JOY!*

Yes, Jesus smiled; yes, Jesus laughed. Jesus smiled bigger and laughed heartier than any human being who's ever walked the planet. It's been revelation to a lot of people both in and out of the church, their eyes opening wide after lifetimes of misunderstanding the Lord to be an aloof, pious, and sanctimonious figure.

One of the most exciting privileges I've had through *Matthew* is seeing teens and kids turning on to Jesus after years of turning their backs on a Savior who had been so tragically misrepresented to them as a stern, anything-but-loving marble statue image. I spoke once to kids in an elementary school. We laughed and talked about Jesus for an hour or so. A few days after the meeting, I received a huge envelope full of homemade greeting cards from the kids. As you can imagine, there was some very funny stuff, but one card in particular really knocked me out. Unlike the others, there were no drawings anywhere, just a simple, three-word sentence written probably a hundred times all across the front. It said, "Jesus is cool! Jesus is cool! Jesus is cool!" And when I opened the card, there it was one last time in huge block letters: JESUS IS COOL!

I'll tell you, if that's the one impression those kids walked away with, I couldn't be more thrilled. And that is simply because it's true—Jesus is "cool." He's not this overbearing, heavy-handed figure waiting for someone to make a wrong move so He can loose a lightning bolt. Quite the contrary! Can't you just see first-century Jesus sitting on a tree stump with a giggling baby girl wrapped in His arms? What a glorious picture! I have no doubt that Jesus would have been giggling and playing and beaming with love for that little girl with all the fullness that God is.

After all, think about how you feel and act with one of your own giggling wonders wrapped in your arms. Can you even begin to measure the way your heart bubbles in a moment like that? How much more the Son of the Living God, whose love for one of His little wonders so dwarfs anything you or I can begin to feel.

As wise and perfect as He was, no one can tell me He would have suppressed all the joy in His heart and sat there insisting on reverence and piety in a moment like that. Jesus had no need to maintain some air of poise, trying to impress people with His holiness. He had no insecurities, and His holiness certainly wasn't wrapped up in outward appearances. He had nothing to prove and no reason to hold back. *He was God,* and He had no problem fully being who He fully was and fully living what He fully felt, every full moment of every full day.

And that word "full" is really how I came to see the joy of Jesus. It wasn't so much just a smile and a laugh, for as hard as He laughed and as big as He smiled, that's how hard He wept and how deeply His heart broke.

The joy of Jesus, I discovered, was wrapped up in His living in all the fullness of life's ultimate adventure—a bigger-than-lifeness, robustness, victoriousness that comes with living 100 percent in the Father's will 100 percent of the time.

Can you imagine the level of joy in your heart if you could live just ten seconds that way? Jesus lived *every breathing* moment that way. It's beyond comprehension! Love unbounded, truth unrestrained, purpose maximized, victory realized, enemy pulverized, humanity eternalized, God glorified—it's just too much to think about.

In fact, would you like to hear a little secret about the joy of Jesus? There's something I've felt strongly every time I've watched *Matthew;*

something I've also felt strongly when I'm all alone with the Lord and finely focused on Him. Are you ready? With all the joy, excitement, and passion Jesus displays in *Matthew*, I don't think we even *remotely* came close! That's just how joyous, exciting, and passionate I believe Jesus truly was 2000 years ago and truly is today. *As far as we went, I don't think we even came close.* There, I said it. Amen.

Yes, joy was to be a cornerstone, and I knew it. But the prospect of having to portray it was very intimidating to me. And one scene in particular had me terrified:

SCENE 3—SEA OF GALILEE SHORE—DAY EXTERIOR

The adult JESUS—walking along a lake shore—turns back and smiles into camera; a clear, brilliant smile; a startling picture.

Let me explain. Both my father and mother are Mediterranean, so I was born with relatively dark features, leaving me pretty much typecast in relatively dark roles. I'd never been asked to play a joyful person, and I wasn't too sure I knew how. Brooding, yes, but joyful—I couldn't picture it. My career was so one-sided that way, I make a little joke that Jesus is the first "nice guy" I ever played.

On top of that, the grinding desert that had been my life for the previous 15 months had drained me of joy. Though excited about *Matthew,* I had been through one long haul and had yet to fully recover from it.

Third (get the tissues out), a few years earlier, I'd been told by someone very close that I should never smile—that, in fact, I was ugly when I smiled. Believe it or not, she intended her comment constructively, in the professional context: "Bruce, don't smile at auditions and you'll get more work because you don't look good when you smile." Good intent aside, those words cut deep. Overnight I pretty much stopped smiling altogether (especially in front of her!), adopting a Dustin Hoffman-style, tight-lipped grin. Consequently I was so tense about having to smile and act joyful in front of that camera, I dove desperately to my knees. "Lord, fill me with Your joy! Dear God, I need it! Put Your smile on my face and in my heart! Do whatever is necessary!" I was begging big-time. The entire production was riding on it.

I can't pick out a day when I woke all full of smiles and filled with joy. I never experienced a moment of manifest release or freedom. All I know is I arrived in Quarzazate smiling so big my face was likely to tear. Excitement was exploding out of my heart, and I was overjoyed to smile as wide and as often as Regardt desired. I was smiling on the set and off the set, in the makeup chair and in the wardrobe room, first thing in the morning and going to sleep at night. There was new life in my heart that drowned that pitiful lie and made those 15 desert months a pale memory. Praise God!

Remember that scene that so terrified me? We shot it one summer evening by a lake in the Cape region of South Africa, as cast and crew were about to break for dinner and the sun was sinking beautifully behind the hills in the distance. Seeing the light was perfect, Regardt called to me, "Bruce, what do you say we shoot that smiling Jesus scene before you eat?"

He dismissed everyone but me, and Tobie, the South African cinematographer. We did a first take, and a second; then Regardt started jumping with excitement. As the three of us walked to the dinner table, he bubbled on and on, "That's one of the best scenes we've shot, brother. I'm telling you, watch and see what the Lord is going to do with that shot alone—I'm telling you!"

Regardt used that scene to close the film—the wind whipping Jesus' cloak and tumbling His hair in a magnificent explosion of life and vitality. Jesus turns, smiles as big as the sun, and tosses a wave in hearty invitation for all to follow. I love it!

And again, Regardt was right. The mountain of testimonies stemming from that one scene, a scene I feared doing, is beyond humbling. It is by far one of the most talked-about moments in *Matthew*. The Lord has used it to knead His love into countless viewing hearts. When He does a thing, He really does a thing!

Another of the most talked-about scenes in the film is Jesus healing the leper. This scene has been the source of so much blessing in people's lives, it blows me away. I'm sad to also report that some—thankfully very few—have chosen to take offense to it. That tears my heart out, because the scene was no clever creation of man, but conceived of the Holy Spirit. And of course the scene's spiritual fruit speaks for itself. Let me tell you how it all came to be.

As it goes, Jesus and His disciples are coursing along a dusty byway fresh from the Sermon on the Mount, and a man with leprosy approaches. "Lord, if You are willing, You can make me clean." Overcome with shame and fear, the poor guy cowers, hiding his diseased face. The crowd disperses in repulsion, but Jesus kneels in the dirt with him, lifting his chin to look into his face.

Brokenhearted, Jesus responds, "I am willing. Be clean." He pulls away the leper's bandages, only to reveal a fresh face—a new man. Realizing what's happened, the man jumps to his feet and explodes in celebration, running wildly through the gasping onlookers.

Suddenly he remembers Jesus—the source of his new life—still kneeling in the dirt. He turns and rushes Him, throwing himself into Jesus' welcome embrace in a magnificent display of unbridled thanksgiving. He knocks Jesus to the ground, smothering Him in affection. The two rejoice together in a roar of laughter. Jesus straightens for a few words, only to be knocked to the ground again in a second explosion of gratitude. End of scene.

Jesus rolling on the ground? Jesus hugging and loving openly? With a filthy leper, of all people? You can see why the scene is so talked about.

But let's set aside presupposed imagery and look at the practicality, the reality, of what actually happened that day. A human being who was drowning in disease, filth, and rejection was suddenly and dramatically freed from it all in the blink of an eye. Wow! Think what that must have meant to the man, not just to be restored health-wise, but to be restored to his family and the society that had booted him out. It doesn't take much to see that this was one gigantic moment in this leper's life. I can't imagine it would have transpired with much calm or reserve. And from Jesus' side, what a thrill to have the opportunity to hand someone a gift like that—to be the source of someone's liberty and renewal, especially someone you love. And it's a thrill Jesus experienced not just this once, but day in and day out—now that's joy!

So where did Reg come up with that scene? Did he have a stroke of creative genius, hoping to turn heads? Let me quote from a magazine interview he did:

> On the set I discovered many new facets of Jesus. I was astounded to see how much "religion" I had inside of me. We were shooting the scene where Jesus healed the leper. I felt compelled by the Lord that Jesus should go on His knees, the healed man should fall into His arms, and together they should roll in the dust. My immediate reaction was, "No, I can't do that!" but obeyed, and that scene became one of the most popular scenes in the whole production. Through the eyes of religion we tend to see Jesus as this extremely reserved and serene figure—the Son of God who would never show so much joy as to burst into laughter and roll in the dust at a leper's healing. But the Lord led us to bring joy to the character of Jesus.

I'll never forget the day we shot that scene. It was late into a blistering South African summer afternoon. Everyone was exhausted, and we could taste the sand between our teeth as the Cape winds whipped it into our faces. The leper was in makeup as Regardt explained the action of the scene to me and the apostles. The actor who played the leper, Tiny Skefile, could not have been more perfectly cast. He stood ready to take a chance at making a complete fool of himself, which is one of the hallmarks of a truly fine actor.

We rehearsed once, and all eyes could see we had a winner. The crew, the extras—everyone out there enjoyed the leper and me rolling around in love and celebration. But we had a logistical problem. For lighting reasons, Jesus would have to approach the leper from one side, then somehow end up on his other side to kneel down and heal him. It was difficult to find a way to make such a move look natural. We had to come up with a believable, human reason for Jesus and the leper to switch sides.

Regardt and I put our heads together and tried a dozen different options, but they all seemed contrived. Finally, after 20 minutes of fruitless brainstorming, we stopped using our heads and started using our knees in prayer. We were 11 hours into a sweltering day and patience was thin among cast and crew, but Reg and I were desperate. We continued to pray for an answer to our dilemma.

Suddenly God dropped it right into our laps. It was as if a lightbulb snapped on, and it was one of those things that is so beautiful and simple: In the presence of his Messiah as well as the surrounding crowd, the leper would be so ashamed of his disfigurement, smell, and all the other humiliation that goes with leprosy, he'd turn away and cover himself. This would force Jesus, who would want to look him in the eye, to circle around and face him, thereby satisfying the cinematographer's lighting requirements in a perfectly believable way.

We put the scene in the can and returned home after a great day's work. Everyone knew something special had been captured—something well worth baking in the sun for. And that simple nuance of the leper cowering, totally orchestrated by the Lord, says so much in terms of humility, repentance, and fear and trembling before God. And it says so much about Jesus in the way He goes out of His way to face this guy and love him, looking right into his darkest ugliness. Added to the expression of joy that ensues, the scene speaks to the hearts of folks across every strata of culture and society. To quote a letter I received, "Never have I seen a Jesus so lovable, gentle, and affectionate. Who couldn't love a Jesus like that!"

And it was all the Lord's idea. Reg is a great director for sure; but the Lord—He's a GREAT director. You've got to love it when *He* bellows "Action!"

———————

Another moment in *Matthew* that opens eyes and melts hearts is when Peter steps out of the boat on the Sea of Galilee. We all know the scene: Jesus walks on the water toward a boat full of apostles. Good old leap-before-you-look Peter calls to Him, "Lord, if it is You, tell me to come to You on the water!" I love the Lord's response—an immediate, straightforward, oh-so-profound "Come!" Peter takes a couple of miraculous steps, then falls into the drink, overwhelmed by fear as the waves swell around him. He cries for help, and Jesus snatches him from peril, saying, "You of little faith, why did you doubt?" Then together they climb into the boat.

Now the thing that has so spoken to people who've seen the film is not so much what Jesus does in the scene as *how* He does it; specifically, how He treats Peter after his plunge into the stormy waters of faithlessness. Jesus joyously, passionately, and lovingly bear-hugs Peter to His chest, belly-laughing in a startling display of affection for His cold, wet, and terrified buddy. It is this show of pleasure and love for Peter in the midst of his seeming failure that astonishes and ministers to people.

You see, the words "You of little faith, why did you doubt?" seem to paint the picture of a stern, scolding Jesus. I've had many people confide to me that every time they've read this passage in the Word, those apparently harsh words have given them trouble. And for good reason. I mean, here is Peter trying so hard to be so good, and when he makes a mistake all Jesus can do is call him names and shake a finger in his face. It sure doesn't seem too forgiving or compassionate. I don't know about anyone else, but if I were Peter, it would make me just want to give up and go back to fishing.

So where did all the joy come from? Was it something we did just to get a laugh? Not a chance! There was one thing I had to keep in mind in everything I did, and it's that one thing that served as the fountainhead of Jesus' overwhelming joy: *He loved people.* It was His mission. It was what He was all about. No matter what He was doing or saying or whom He was dealing with, it was a constant that had to be fundamental to my *every* action while the camera was rolling.

Oh, how deeply Jesus must have loved Peter, and not only as his Lord. Can you imagine the specific affection He must have had for this simple fisherman who so completely adored Him and would do anything for Him—even step off a boat? Jesus never would have done a thing to push Peter away. It would have been completely contrary to His mission, His character, and their relationship.

Try to picture what Peter must have looked like to Jesus that night—this charmingly bullheaded man climbing over the rail of a boat in the middle of a storm, blinded with devotion and wonder. Can you imagine the surge of affection Jesus must have felt as He watched this beloved friend take that against-all-reason leap of faith—this Peter whose intentions were the purest of pure; this Peter who was trying so hard; this Peter who was caught being so lovably human; this Peter who was just so "Peter."

I wasn't there that night in history, but I have no doubt that love for Peter was pouring from Jesus' eyes like a waterfall. I bet He was thrilled with excitement and joy unbounded as He watched this grown man— this delightfully bumbling man—come to Him so completely as He would have every one of us come to Him: *as a child.* And it wasn't a love reserved for only those moments when Peter did good. It wasn't a love hidden or held back. It was a love simply, entirely, and constantly poured out, even when the object of that love messed up.

Has someone you dearly love ever made a mess of things in an effort to please you? I have a friend whose son has a learning disability. One thing this child so loves to do is make her breakfast in bed. She says he walks into her room well before the alarm, excitedly wakes her, and plops down a tray full of burnt toast, half-cooked egg, and cold coffee, along with a single daisy floating in a drinking glass. She says it's the worst-tasting breakfast anyone could imagine, but she gladly eats every bite because *to her heart* it tastes as if it came from the finest gourmet kitchen. She wouldn't trade that burnt toast for anything in the world, and it's all she can do to hold back tears of joy as she looks into his trying-so-hard face in spite of the failed efforts spread across her plate.

We've all had that kind of experience on one level or another; we've all felt that surge of love for some clumsy someone who tried so hard. And if that's how we who are so completely imperfect feel at a time like that—if that's the rush of joy that floods into our hearts—how much more the Son of the Living God!

I will never forget standing on that stormy lake watching Herrit Schoonoven, our Peter, step out of the boat. Herrit brought a sweet vulnerability, a trying-too-hard awkwardness to Peter that is refreshing compared to the stereotypical man's man Peter is generally pictured to be.

As the wind was howling and the waves were pounding, I stood on a platform sunk just below the surface watching "Peter" tentatively step over the rail. He looked so wonderfully clumsy, pushing over one leg, then the other, my heart just leaped with affection. Excitement filled me as I watched, in character, this man take a truly remarkable step of faith. And when danger got the better of him and he went down, oh, how much more my heart surged with the victory and comedy of it all. As I pulled him up and clutched him to my chest, I couldn't help but roar with affection. My script notes on the scene contain only three simple words: "Enjoy him thoroughly." And enjoy him, I did.

A little behind-the-scenes story: Herrit has little vision without his glasses. When he stepped out of the boat, he could hardly see where the platform under the water began or ended. In fact, on one take he actually missed it and fell into the water. Because he couldn't see well, he was very unsure of himself, just staring blankly into nothingness throughout the sequence. As awful as that sounds, it registered magnificently on film and brought a precious sense of innocence and awe to what surely would have been such a moment in Peter's history. Don't you just love the way the Lord uses those kinds of things to His glory?

Before we go on, I must tell you, you've just got to pick up a copy of *Jesus, Man of Joy*. I've read it cover to cover many times following that rain-soaked night I first saw it. And during the *Matthew* shoot, whenever I felt dry as an actor, I'd read it through before the night-light went out. The next day I'd walk onto the set freshly grounded in the blessed reality that Jesus was indeed a Man of Joy.

I just now flipped through a few pages of it and realized that in this chapter I'm writing, I could add nothing to what its respected author, Sherwood Wirt, has already penned. Let me quote a bit from him:

> He was young. He radiated good cheer. . . . The *real* [there's that word, again] Jesus, a man of such merriment, such gladness of spirit, such freedom and openness, that He was irresistible . . . a keen sense of humor . . . filled with eagerness and anticipation. A dazzling display of love . . . He set hearts afire . . . an incredible quality of life. An elated, triumphant young man . . . His happy, radiant, loving personality, so different from the solemn religious types He constantly encountered.

Like I said—Jesus, *Man of Joy*.

You know, I'm looking right now at my binder full of research notes I carried with me on the shoot. It's open to the front page—a page I stuck up front so it would hit my eyes first thing.

Along the left side is a string of 17 words in a vertical column. The afternoon I scribbled them, I was buried in my research and feeling overwhelmed, thinking, *How am I possibly going to convey everything that Jesus is?*

Being the lover of simplicity I am, I closed all my reference books and sat back with a clean sheet of paper, and a prayer. After a moment with the Lord, I decided to list 15 specific terms that characterize Jesus—not typical terms like "glorious" or "loving" but more graphic, tangible things I could grab hold of in my imagination.

The first eight or so came pretty easy, but the next six or seven took some digging, and finally a couple more popped into mind as icing on the cake. It seemed the more I pushed and the deeper I dug—*the more I pressed into Jesus*—the more specific and revealing the descriptions got, until the final one, which bottom-lines everything. The list reads:

> Pure, Solid, Miraculous, Permanent, Sweet, Fresh, Vibrant, Never weary, Big, Intimate, Born of the heart, True, With ease, Clean, Electric, Creative, *For other people.*

What more can I say? Jesus was a man of excitement, a man of giving, a man of living, a *MAN OF JOY.*

And the joy He lived was so much more than just a sunburst smile; it was a joy that lived and breathed in a fullness of passion founded in desperate love and celebrated in everything He said and did. It was a joy whose ultimate expression was not a robust belly laugh, though belly-laugh He did, but rather a trio of nails through the hands and feet; for as the book of Hebrews puts it, "For the *joy* set before Him [He] endured the cross."

Joy. Not as the world knows it, but as He defined it—living, breathing, walking, dying—Jesus the Christ . . .

MAN OF JOY

Pure
Solid
Miraculous
Permanent
Sweet
Fresh
Vibrant
Never weary
Big
Intimate
Balm of the heart
True
Ease
Clean
Electric
Creative
For other people

Bruce — go on a
mission of love!

A mission &
purpose of redemptive
love

Pour out
my heart &
compassion onto
everyone

Love these people

Bruce
Drown
them w/love

① all communications
are heart to heart

② Every word/action is
for other people

③ Mission is to show
this heart of goodness toward
all
— to bleed from the
heart for all to see
— to allow people to
look into His eyes &
touch His face.
— to reach out to all

Bruce ① go on a mission
of love — actually minister

② choose Jesus in
my off time
— stay close by
His side &
looked from all
that is not of H
③ Become the character
— Jesus was always
completely concerned
away from self

ON A MISSION OF REDEMPTIVE LOVE

That you ... may be able to comprehend with all the saints what is the width and length and depth and height—to know the love of Christ, which passes knowledge.

EPHESIANS 3:18,19

*O*N A MISSION OF REDEMPTIVE LOVE." I will never forget the first time I saw those words printed in *Jesus, Man of Joy.* They shot off the page and exploded in my heart like skyrockets. The moment I laid eyes on them, I knew I'd discovered what we actors call the "through-line" of Jesus Christ: the character's essence and core, from which his everything branches. Al, that acting coach of mine, used to call it the character's "spine"—what it is that propels him through life, founds his choices and priorities, and steers his every action and word. In other words, *what it is that lies at the root of who he is.*

It was the "Master key" to unlocking Jesus' character/personality, and without it, I didn't stand a chance of playing Him accurately or effectively. So from the onset I hunted and prayed desperately for it.

Then suddenly one evening, with my feet on my desk and the dog snoring beside me, there it was in black and white, screaming from that little paperback—six words from which would cascade everything I did as Jesus in *Matthew:* "On a mission of redemptive love," the bottom line of all Jesus came for and all He did.

His every move, every word, every healing, every rebuke, every drop of blood—*an act of love!* From the moment He lay in the manger to the day He disappeared behind the clouds—all acts of love. Jesus, the Christ, the Son of the Living God—simply, purely, completely, and unshakably on a mission of redemptive love! I will never forget my heart skipping double-time when I saw those words, reading them again and again, scribbling and highlighting them. I will never forget diving into the Gospel and suddenly seeing it everywhere. It was a deluge pouring from every paragraph of every page: Jesus just plain loving people. And so, for the first time in my life, I sat down to take a focused look at this "love of Jesus" I'd been hearing about ever since I was old enough to hear. I sat down to explore what it was, what it meant, what it looked like and acted like, what it felt like, and how it was lived by Jesus as He walked the shores of Galilee 2000 years ago.

Oh, what a surprise lay in store! Every day at my desk, every day on the set was a lifetime of uncovering treasures of indescribable passion, care, and giving beyond giving. With all I'd previously known; with all the sermons I'd heard and all the hymns I'd sung, I knew *nothing.*

The intimacy, the devotion, the heart-cry, the eye-to-eye attention, the purity, the *passion*—so much more than any of us can wrap our minds around. Love manifest and poured out in its fullness of expression. An explosion of unbridled involvement so opposite the stereotype of an aloof and mystical Christ with arms outstretched and eyes locked heavenward.

I'm talking about a look in the eye that would burn holes through granite and a life-sacrificing, no-holds-barred passion. I'm talking about heart-melting, hug-smothering affection. To paraphrase the apostle Paul (a far better authority than I), I'm talking "so wide, so deep, so long, so high *it surpasses knowledge.*"

There's an old Jesus movie of decades ago entitled *The Greatest Story Ever Told.* I used to think that was the ultimate title for a Jesus movie. But after touching on His life like I did, I've come to realize that even this title falls far short of the mark. The story of Jesus—His life, death, and resurrection—is not the greatest story ever told, but the greatest *love story* ever told.

Remember the leper scene? Jesus is walking along a dirt road, fresh from what was undoubtedly an exhausting Sermon on the Mount. He'd spent the day, maybe the week, surrounded by soul-hungry, needy people—each one crying for His attention, clinging, demanding, questioning. Can you imagine the noise, the mob confusion, the humanity pressing in? And again, first-century reality was a far cry from those Renaissance paintings where all of creation sits frozen in reverence while Jesus pontificates. This was real life and these were real people—and not, by and large, the sophisticated, well-mannered, upper crust of Galilean society. They were the "tax collectors and sinners"—not exactly the kind of folks who are going to sit quietly and wait their turn.

And it wasn't just the people who were real; the elements and conditions were real as well. Can you imagine Jesus' sun- and wind-parched face, His cotton-dry mouth after an entire day of teaching in the open air, belting out His glorious truths over the camels and goats and whatever else was roaming the countryside? Can you imagine His aching feet, His fatigue, His human craving for a cool bath or even just a wet rag to wipe the sting of sand and dust from His eyes? Or His human longing for an hour of quiet and solitude out of the sun and away from the crowds? Again, Jesus lived a very real life, and any honest look paints a picture of our Lord that's as hard-lived and down-to-earth as real life gets.

With all that swirling around Him, Jesus comes down from the Mount and presses toward Capernaum. Suddenly there is a muffled cry, "Lord, if you are willing, you can make me clean." Jesus turns to see a man, filthy and wretched, face shielded behind strips of grimy linen. It's a man everyone else is running from and shouting at—a man with leprosy.

The leper—a personality who's become so familiar and almost romanticized as we read his story, picking it apart for spiritual truth. But you know, I discovered something on the set that is so obvious it feels almost silly to say. Because of that, it's probably the most missed aspect of the story, yet it's as significant a truth to understand and embrace as there is:

This leper, 2000 years ago was a *very real person.*

He wasn't a character in some story, or even a device set up by God to teach future generations. When Jesus turned around that day, what stared Him in the face was a living, breathing *human being.* A man with a name and history; hopes, dreams, and desires; a mother, father, maybe even a wife and kids—I don't know. All I know is he was very, very *real.*

And so was his leprosy. Have you ever laid eyes on a leper? It's a horrific sight, as repugnant to behold as our imaginations can begin to grasp. Leprosy manifests itself in physical mutilation and deterioration. The skin, the face—everything bursts in sores and open wounds, festering with bleeding and infection. Chunks of flesh die and fall away, bone turns to chalk. Can you imagine the filth, the disease, the smell, the ugliness? Can you imagine the anguish, the shame, the rejection, the aloneness, the hopelessness—can you imagine this leper? He would have been removed from society, forced to leave his wife and family to live in the wilderness. I'm telling you, this guy was oozing with sickness and despised because of it. He was spit on, turned away, and avoided. No one wanted this guy around. They all just wished he would go off and die somewhere.

That's who this leper was 2000 years ago. Yet one day Jesus, *the Son of the Living God*—and if anyone has important things to do, it's the Son of the Living God—stopped everything He was doing and turned all His attention on *this guy*, this guy everyone else was throwing rocks at.

Scripture doesn't exactly specify, but I don't believe for one second that Jesus struck some pose of what we would consider godly dignity above this fellow. Which of us, if we saw one of our own children in such pain, would respond with something like that? Not a one! We would rush to his side, throw ourselves onto the ground, take him into our arms, weep for his agony, and cry to God for him. There isn't one of us who would care a lick about reverence in a moment like that, or getting our clothes dirty, or what people might think.

If that is how all-out you and I would love our own child in a moment like that, how much more the Son of God, whose love is so far beyond what you or I can even begin to approach? How much more the Son of the Living God, who is the very personification of everything love is, ever has been, or ever can be?

You see, He *created* that leper. He knew that leper's name—He *named* that leper. He hand-knit that leper in his mother's womb. In other words—

That leper 2000 years ago was *His very own child.*

That's the specific relationship; *that's* the specific love; *that's* the specific intimacy.

I don't have children, so I can't imagine the specific heart of a parent for a child—I can only hook into the feeling I have for my family and nephews and niece. But if you have children, imagine the way you feel about your kids, multiply it a billion times, and you're *possibly* beginning to come close to the heart of Jesus for that leper that day.

No, I have no doubt Jesus would have gotten right down in the dirt with that guy, taking him into His arms, slipping a gentle, calloused hand under that diseased chin, pulling away his mask of rags, and smiling into his shame-filled face. Yes, the Jesus I discovered would have reached a finger right into one of those hideous wounds, wept with that guy, grieved over his brokenness, ached over his pain, held him, and wiped away his every tear.

And with words so simple, so intimate, so sure—words whispered deep into that leper's eyes as if there was no one there but the two of them: "I am willing; *be clean.*" And that leper *was* clean—in a heartbeat, snatched from disease, despair, shame, and rejection—fully and completely *a new creation.* Praise His glorious Name!

And here's the big key: He doesn't love that leper any more or differently than He loves anyone on this planet—"He is not a respecter of persons." As I said earlier, take the way you feel about your own flesh-and-blood child (or if you have no kids, whoever you love the most), multiply it a billion times, and you're *possibly beginning* to come close to how Jesus felt about that leper that day and you're possibly beginning to come close to how He feels about *you* today. He loves you; He loves you *so much*. Embrace it, friend—it's truth like there is no truth.

And women—oh, how He treasures and honors you. That's one of the surprise discoveries I made about Jesus. We hear so much about His special heart for kids, but I discovered Jesus had a special heart of care for women as well. Mary Magdalene is a good example. Even more than the leper, she's a Bible personality so familiar to us all and so largely glamourized we tend to lose awareness of who this very real woman truly was.

In art Mary Magdalene always seems to be a graceful, adoring beauty, usually dressed in flowing blues and silken reds. Sometimes she even comes equipped with her own shimmering halo. But that was not Mary Magdalene's reality 2000 years ago—not even close. Scripture never states outright she was a prostitute; it implies she was one. What it does state specifically is that Jesus cast seven demons out of her. Wow! With seven demons, prostitute or not, this woman must have been a mess. Let's say she was a prostitute, as most scholars believe she was. If you can, try to imagine what that means about what Mary *did* every day of her life. Two, three, four, maybe five different guys in a day doing whatever they pleased to her, then walking out and leaving her to clean up their wreckage. Maybe one would beat her around just for kicks. Maybe sometimes they'd just refuse to pay, laughing and slamming the door behind them as she lay naked, filthy, and used.

Imagine the infection that must have run rampant through her body with violation upon violation. Imagine the pain that would slice her heart when the very man she'd just given herself to strolled by with a secure, smiling wife neatly tucked under his arm. Imagine the depth of rejection as he sees her and turns the other way. Imagine Mary's face—hard and sallow, weathered and drawn with years of being used and thrown away by the hands of brutal men. Imagine the shame, the loneliness, the anger, the self-hatred, the hardness—the utter deadness of spirit, soul, and body. If there was ever a woman treated like dirt, who'd thrown away her every shred of womanhood, if there was ever a woman who hated herself and everyone around her, it would have been this woman.

Now, history doesn't record the moment, but there came a day when Mary Magdalene finally encountered a Real Man, a man who would look her in the eye and with a single glance say, "You're valuable. You're special. I know because I'm the God who molded you— I did it with My own two hands. Your name lives in My heart. I don't care what you've done or how many times you've done it. I don't care how hard your heart is or how wrecked your body is. I am your Way, your Truth, and your Life, and I will *never* leave you nor forsake you. In my eyes you're as beautiful a creature as I've ever had the pleasure of creating, and I love you—*just the way you are.*"

Yes, Mary Magdalene finally met a "real" man. I can't tell you where they were that day or what they said to each other. Maybe they were in the marketplace, and some self-righteous merchant was chasing her from his produce: "Take your business elsewhere, wicked woman!" Maybe they met on the street, and someone yelled to Jesus, "Rabboni! Destroy that filthy whore!" Maybe Mary washed His feet with her tears. I have no idea. But I do know that Jesus felt about Mary just as He felt about that leper: *She was His child,* His baby, *and His baby was in pain.* And I can't help but imagine that, as with that leper, Jesus got right down on her level, and looked her square in the eye, and reached a strong hand to wipe her every tear away, and smiled into her battered face.

I can't help but see, in that shower of love, Mary collapsing with emotion and relief, her shoulders shaking in His embrace as her heart, so scarred and battered, begins to feel life for the first time since she was a little girl. And Jesus, her newfound Savior, on His knees crying with her, wrapping His own shawl around her. "Take heart, daughter. Be clean."

And I see Peter, John, and all the others looking on with tears streaming down their leathered cheeks as they witness this display of love that is so far beyond any definition of love they ever dreamed possible; and all of it poured out on one who ranks among the most unlovable. A love that is so humble, so unashamed—so *Jesus*.

I wasn't there that day, and I may be so far off base it isn't funny. All I know is that's the love I discovered pulsating in His heart, pouring from His eyes, and spilling from His touch. *Jesus*.

As I write about these things, I'm reminded of an evening some companions and I ministered in an orphanage outside Bloemfontein, South Africa. It was a bare-bones, penniless, forgotten operation in the middle of a bare-bones, penniless, forgotten township. The conditions were hard to look at, and even harder to smell, but still miles above what those children would face on the street.

After we spoke to the kids, we prayed for them one by one. It was all very hard on our hearts. These kids had tasted more atrocity in their few years than any dozen people should taste in a hundred lifetimes. I was barely hanging on to my emotions the whole evening.

One of my partners was a rugged young guy named Thomas, a strong, zealous kid of about 20 who reminded me of Simon Peter—raw and "out there," and not the most sophisticated guy in the world; but what a burning love for Jesus and compassion for lost and hurting people he had. This was Thomas' first ministry outreach experience.

A little girl in a dirty pink T-shirt went to him for prayer. She was about 12, and like the other kids, she had lived a tale of woe no one should ever have been subjected to, let alone this barefoot beauty. The woman who ran the orphanage told me her story: One day when she was eight, she'd skipped home from school only to find her mother and father gone. The night came and went, the next day came and went, and the next day, and the next. There was no note, no message with a neighbor, nothing—they were just gone. Four years had passed, and that little girl was still hoping, still waiting every day for her mom and dad to come home.

Well, Thomas no sooner began to pray for her than her huge brown eyes filled with tears; and as Thomas continued, she completely broke down, shaking and collapsing into his arms. Thomas broke down right along with her. He fell to his knees, weeping and praying, holding her skinny little frame to his chest. He clutched her as tightly as he could, as if to squeeze the pain out of her.

Thomas held that little girl like that for a good hour. There was no way he was going to abandon her, no matter how long she needed him to hold her. Finally she cried herself out and just hung in his embrace. To be held like that, to feel loved—it was the whole world to her.

We began to leave around 11:30 P.M. As I was saying goodbye to the staff and kids, Thomas was still on his knees, holding and loving that girl. Barely awake and limp with fatigue, she was finally lifted out of his arms and carried to bed. Thomas remained there by himself for the longest time, his face blotched, his T-shirt soaked with sweat and tears. Eventually he rose to his feet and silently made his way to the car where everyone was waiting.

I can't speak for what anyone else was thinking that night, but as I looked at Thomas collapsed on the floor, clinging to that little girl, *I saw Jesus.* I saw Jesus with the leper; I saw Jesus with Mary Magdalene; I saw Jesus with me. I just plain saw Jesus.

In *Matthew,* one acting problem I remember was the Pharisees: How would Jesus have dealt with them? The answer hit home when we were on location at Theewaterskloof Dam (our South African Sea of Galilee) preparing to shoot a scene where the Pharisees confront Jesus about violating the Sabbath. One would immediately picture the scene as a high-noon showdown, but Regardt was much too insightful to shoot it so predictably. Instead he shot it on a long lens, making it visually one of the softest scenes in the film—Jesus and the Pharisees strolling the graceful Galilean shoreline.

Generally, older men played our Pharisees, and they were in real life warm and great fun. That afternoon they were so excited, just laughing and chatting with each other as they got into costume. By pure coincidence, I was sitting at a distance, sipping my coffee and watching them. It was so sweet a sight, but then suddenly it hit me:

Jesus *loved* the Pharisees. I mean, he *really* loved them! It didn't matter that they bad-mouthed Him, plotted against Him, hated Him, and would eventually kill Him. Certainly He despised their sin, but nonetheless He loved them.

And in that love, His every action toward them would be no different from His every action toward anyone else. After all, He created those Pharisees just as He created you, me, the leper, and Mary Magdalene: They too were His kids. And it didn't make a difference how many times they laughed in His face or slapped away His invitation, He would keep coming back. He came to *save* the lost, not push them away—no matter who they were or what their crimes may have been. "I love you! Come to Me!"

One of our Pharisees was a bit feeble and had weak legs. As a result, the sand and gravel by the lake proved difficult for him to maneuver. But as the scene developed in rehearsal, it hit me—Jesus, a young, vital man, seeing this old fellow struggle, would undoubtedly help him. It was so obvious—Jesus loved the guy, and to help him along would be His *natural reaction.* And what a perfect opportunity for Jesus to *show* love to the guy, winning him over with love not just talked about but *lived* and *demonstrated.*

The cameras rolled, and we began our stroll. As I spoke with the men, I slipped my left arm around this Pharisee's waist, supporting him with my right, helping him every step of the way. What ended up on film is revelation—Jesus in an open display of affection for a man who absolutely *hated* Him. Jesus, literally and actively *loving His enemy,* as He'd so preached.

As the scene goes on, Jesus stops, looks them all in the eye, and joyously declares, "One greater than the temple is here!" as if to say, "I'm for real, guys. And like it or not, I love you like you can't imagine!" Our Pharisees were completely taken aback. They knew their job was to be antagonistic, and they assumed they'd be met with the same; but when they saw gentleness coming their way, they just melted. I could see it on their faces—they just stood listening with wide eyes and open hearts, completely disarmed and amazed.

Bruce Rudnick was watching the action unfold from a nearby bluff. He would tell me afterward that he was casually looking on, then suddenly he saw it—a sight so stunning, so true—Jesus loving the very man who would call for his death. Bruce told me he couldn't believe his eyes, and at the same time he couldn't believe he'd never before considered it. Half in excitement and half in shock, he said to me, "It was so lovely, my brother, and so right. It was *revelation.*" No, my brother—it was love; it was Jesus.

And then there was Judas. In the film, during the Last Supper, Judas whispers to Jesus, "Surely not I, Rabbi?" and Jesus breaks in heartache, taking Judas' face in His hands, burying His head into his shoulder, squeezing the words through emotion and tears, "Yes, it is you." I can't tell you how often I'm asked where that reaction came from.

I remember thinking Jesus' relating to Judas would be one of my biggest acting challenges. How would Jesus have interacted with this man, aware all along of the darkness in his heart; aware the day would come when this man would sell Him for 30 bucks? Surely from the moment they met, Jesus looked into Judas' eyes and saw betrayal—He saw the cross.

Scripture doesn't tell us very much about Judas. We know he handled the money and skimmed some off the top; we know he killed himself. So much is debated—did he go to heaven or hell? Was he predestined to what he did, or did he choose it? And what was his problem with Jesus—was he greedy, jealous, or what?

We tend to picture Judas as a conniving, crooked-nosed crumb of a man. There's a theory that he was a political zealot who in the betrayal was actually trying to force Jesus into using His power to take the throne. That would explain his response to the horrific events that followed, as well as the apparent contradictions in so many of his actions—the kiss, the immediate confession, the suicide. On the other hand, many think Judas was just an opportunistic little man who'd sell his own grandmother if the price was right.

I don't know myself. It would be easy to write him off as an avaricious creep, but I have a feeling it wasn't that way at all. I can't help but think Judas was nothing more than just a little too human, if you know what I mean. I can't help but think he was just a bit confused, impatient, fearful, proud, and ambitious—in other words, your

101

everyday kind of guy. I can't help but think Judas, just like the leper and Mary Magdalene, was nothing other than very, very real.

So how would Jesus have related to Him? I labored many hours over this one. But you know, it was so simple, so incredibly obvious. I was reading John 13, where Jesus washes the apostles' feet—He's the Son of the Living God and He gets down on the ground and washes these guys' dirty feet. Why? Verse one gives the reason: "He now showed them the full extent of His love;" *Love,* to a group of 12 guys, ten of whom would desert Him in His time of greatest need, and one of whom would sell Him for a pocketful of loose change.

Guess whose dirty feet were right in there with the rest of them? Judas. The Son of God got down on the floor and, without a whisper, scrubbed the dirt off the same feet that would guide a pack of murderers to Him in a handful of hours. Why would Jesus do that? To show Judas the full extent of His love.

In filming the Last Supper, Judas, masterfully played by David Minaar, was sitting to my right. I'll never forget seeing him reach in front of me to dip his bread into the water bowl and me rushing my hand into the same bowl to meet it: "The one who has dipped his hand into the bowl with me will betray me." He just froze; and then, "Surely not I, Rabbi?"

That tore my heart to shreds. Here was this guy walking straight into his own destruction. He'd had every chance a man could have, and here he was, signing not just Jesus' death warrant, but *his own.* Emotionally, I just lost it. I grabbed his face, burying my head into his shoulder, grieving, "Yes, it is you."

David's eyes filled with tears in that moment. Then he pried my hand off his face and pushed me away. I never outright asked him— it's one of those things you just don't ask an actor—but I don't think for one second those tears were him "acting" at all.

But yes, folks, Jesus was passionate for even this guy. He was passionate in reaching out even for Judas.

You know, all during the shoot, tiny phrases from Scripture I'd read a thousand times would suddenly leap off the page as if I were seeing

them for the very first time. One of those little phrases completely redesigned my perception of Jesus and the love He's dying (or should I say, *died*) to give me. Most of us know the story. Jesus is doing His usual—pouring buckets of truth on the hungry hearts of ancient Judea. Suddenly a voice in the crowd belts out the $25,000 question: "Who is the greatest in the kingdom of heaven?"

I can picture a Pharisee primping himself to receive his "well-deserved" honors—or maybe Peter, clearing his throat for an impromptu acceptance speech. I hear a rumble of hushed speculation flow through the crowd: "Moses!" "Elijah!" "No, it's Jeremiah!" And the buzz of anticipation: "Who will Rabboni choose?" "Who is the greatest?"

There's no way I can vouch for what anyone may have expected from Jesus in reply, but I guarantee it was nothing close to what they received. Their collective jaws must have dropped to the ground when Jesus turned, called a little boy to His side, and spoke a sentence that blasts centuries of stained-glass sophistication right through the roof:

> Unless you *change and become like little children,*
> you will never enter the kingdom of heaven.
> Therefore, whoever humbles himself like this child
> is the greatest in the kingdom of heaven.

I remember noticing it while I was in L.A. preparing. It so struck me, I ran down to the local park to sit and watch. What I saw there I'd seen countless times, but oh, what I learned—*He wants me to come to Him as one of these.* Wide-eyed, dirty-faced, barefooted, openhearted; with a hug, not a handshake; with a nuzzle, not a notebook; with a giggle, not a grovel—*as a child.*

Recently I sat in Regardt's living room watching Disney cartoons with his four-year-old son, David, and two of his playmates. One of those playmates was a six-year-old girl, the daughter of a farm worker. As she strolled into the room, there were a dozen places she could have chosen to sit, but she walked over and plunked down alongside me. Then, without batting an eyelash, she leaned in and curled under my arm, nestling into my chest.

I can't put into words how that took my breath away. It was so astoundingly unsophisticated, unintimidated, unpretentious, void of formality, needing, trusting, vulnerable, fearless, and given-over. And the God who created heaven and earth whispers into my heart, "Come to Me *as one of these.*"

If we could only grasp that it's that personal, that heartfelt to Him. If we could only hear His heartcry: "The kingdom of heaven belongs to such as these. Change and become like one of these!" It's the very thing the tax collectors and prostitutes and sinners grasped so long ago, and it's that very thing the Pharisees and teachers of the law so tragically missed. Oh, how passionate He is; how desperate and longing for us to understand, to reach out, to know, to come and come and come some more, and just curl into His huge embrace, and just love Him—*as a child.*

You know, I find myself thinking of that card, "Jesus is cool!" It came from a kid, maybe eight or nine years old—no reputation to uphold, no superdoctrine to fight for, no years of emotional dulling, no grand vision to pursue . . . in other words, none of that grown-up stuff. All that kid knows is what is fun and what isn't; all that kid has is heart—probably a lot like the little boy who stood alongside his Messiah 2000 years ago and heard himself proclaimed to be a model of the greatest in the kingdom of heaven.

I never thought of it until now, but I bet when that little fellow felt Jesus' sure hand settle on his shoulder, heard the words that came out of His divine mouth, and saw the shock sweep across the crowd—I bet, in that moment, he just kind of looked up at Jesus and thought to himself, "You know, this Jesus-guy is pretty cool for a grownup. Yeah, *Jesus is cool.*"

Recently I chatted with a friend who'd given her grandmother a copy of *Matthew* for a Christmas gift. This granny is one of those longstanding Christian ladies now living alone in a convalescent home somewhere in Maine. Her granddaughter told me, "She sits in front of the television watching *Matthew*, and just cries and cries and cries . . . "

When I heard that story, I got a little choked up myself, and Jesus' words once again warmed my heart: "For the kingdom of heaven belongs to such as these." I remember thinking, *She gets it. That little old granny gets it.*

You know, I get asked a lot, "What's the most significant thing you learned through the whole adventure? What discovery stands above the rest?" It may sound crazy, but it's something I'd been hearing all my life. Funny thing is, I don't know that I ever truly heard it, or perhaps I heard it so much I lost all sense of what it truly is. But I'm going to tell you right now what that most significant thing is, and I want you to hear it as if for the very first time in your life. I want you to close your ears and listen with your heart. I want you to let it sink in and find a very deep place, never to be uprooted, not ever. Because, I have to tell you, it's the only thing that will be left standing when all is said and done. That one thing I learned; that single most significant discovery?

He loves you.

He loves you *so much.*

It doesn't matter who you are, or how many mistakes you've made, or what anyone thinks of you, or what you may think of yourself. It doesn't matter if you doubt it, laugh at it, or if you love it. There's nothing you can do to change it or make it go away, and it's as real as the ink on this page:

He loves you.

Jesus.

"IT KILLS HIM, REG. IT JUST KILLS HIM."

CHAPTER SEVEN

When he saw the crowds, he had compassion on them, because they were harassed and helpless, like sheep without a shepherd.

MATTHEW 9:36

FOLLOWING THE SOUTH AFRICAN release of *Matthew* I toured that country for an amazing six months, first in promotion, then in ministry. My life during that time was the living definition of on-the-run: eating in restaurants, shaving on airplanes, sleeping in hotel rooms, and changing clothes in the car.

I remember one day in Bloemfontein actually doing a record nine meetings that stretched from morning to night. And then there was the Sunday I spoke in two different Durban churches, flew to Pretoria for an afternoon stadium event, then back to Durban for an evening service. It was madness, and it was glorious. I made a lot of friends, had a lot of fun, shed a lot of tears, and saw God touch a lot of lives. What a privilege it was, and as Regardt so eloquently puts it, "That's what it's all about, my 'Bru.'"

But as you can imagine, time to sit quietly alone with the Lord was hard to find. Most often it came in the afternoons when I'd try to nap before the inevitable evening meeting, setting the alarm 15 minutes early just to have that quiet time over a hearty supper of Holiday Inn instant coffee—*M-m-m-m good!*

It was during one of those quiet times I was reading Exodus 34—the Lord comes to Moses, passes before him, proclaims His name, and describes Himself. If I'd read the passage once, I'd read it a hundred times, but for some reason, for the first time in my life I "saw" it. God passes by Moses, proclaiming His name and *describing Himself.* Think about that for a moment—this was not a preacher describing God, or a teacher, writer, denomination, artist, or even an actor! This was *God* describing God.

This was God saying, "This is who I am"; this was a portrait of God painted by God; this was God on God—straight from the source, no middle man.

Now I don't know how that strikes you, but that day it really grabbed my attention. I mean, God was shooting straight from the hip here, and I didn't want to miss any of it. So I shook myself awake and read it. Then I read it again—and again. And my mind got blown sky-high.

What's the first term you'd use to describe God? I have to think most of us would immediately come up with something big like *all-powerful, exalted, all-knowing.* Let me ask as well—what do you think is the first word God would use to describe Himself, as He did for Moses that day? What do you think is the first thing God wanted Moses to know about Him? Again, I figure most would guess the same big kinds of things—*glorious, majestic,* and so on.

How about *compassionate?* According to my NIV translation, the first thing God wanted Moses to know about Him that day—and I have to assume He put it at the top of the list for a good reason—was that He was compassionate.

I was stunned that afternoon, and I still am to this day. The Lord goes on to describe Himself further as "gracious," "slow to anger," "abounding in love," "abounding in faithfulness," "maintaining love to thousands," "forgiving," and finally (paraphrased), "just". Astounding!

Every one, a matter of the *heart!* But as I sat in that hotel room with the sun setting over some South African city whose name I can't recall, out of all those characteristics, it was that very first one—compassion—and the priority given it, that leaped off the page more than any other. It took me back to a cold winter day in a Quarzazate marketplace, when I learned the true definition—His—of that word for the first time in my life.

———————

It was just the second day of the shoot. I had traipsed through the desert the day before, which went incredibly well, but the challenges I presently faced made those victories feel like a distant memory. Little did I know at the time, but the experience that would accompany those challenges would make just about everything in my entire life feel like a distant memory.

Let me start by saying this is a very difficult story to tell. It's hard on my heart, as it carries a flood of emotions in a depth I never knew existed before that day. The story also hits me so square in the face with, *What are you doing with your life, Bruce?* that every time I recall it I cringe to think of the time I've tossed away on less-than-important pursuits.

It's also the story of an experience that has carried with it great cost as well as great value. You see, following that second day and what went with it, the Lord has never looked the same to me, I haven't looked the same to me, and nothing and nobody in the entire world have looked the same to me. One side of that is excitement beyond excitement, but the other side is heartache like I never knew before. Now there are times I can barely watch CNN without losing my emotions. I can hardly speak in front of an audience without doing the same. Sometimes I'm sitting at a red light and someone will walk by on the sidewalk, and I'll start to lose it. In short, it's made the day-in, day-out living of ordinary life in an "ordinary" world a bit difficult for me.

Another reason the story is difficult to tell is that it can sound "out there" to some folks. I don't know how you feel, but whenever some guy goes on about how he was driving in his car and the Lord appeared in his backseat and gave him a special message or whatever, as much as I believe that stuff happens, there's a part of me that wonders if

111

maybe this guy didn't just get hold of some bad Chinese food. I mean, if anyone believes the Holy Spirit does supernatural things in our natural world, it's me; but for the most part, for whatever reason, as much as I'd love to be swimming in a sea of such experiences, they just don't seem to come my way. And that's all I can really tell you by way of providing some measure of confidence in the veracity of the story I'm about to share. But as with any spiritual message, check it against the Word of God for yourself. Don't ever take my word or anyone else's for any of it!

But more than these considerations, the story is most difficult to tell simply because I don't have adequate words. The depth and breadth of what happened out there that day is so far beyond my ability to describe that every time I make an attempt, whether it be in an interview or for an audience, I walk away frustrated at my inability. All I've ever been able to do—and that's all I can do here as well—is do what I can with the vocabulary I have and trust the Holy Spirit to work in spite of my stumblings.

As I mentioned, it was only the second day of the shoot. The cast and crew were all in that warm-up stage of feeling each other out and trying to fit into an effective team. As for me, there was no time to indulge in that stage. I had my first lengthy speaking scene that morning, and it was weighing heavy on my mind. Rolling around the desert like we were the day before was one thing, but this would be the real test. Whether we had an eight- or a fourteen-hour day rested squarely on my ability to not just act the speech word for word, but act it well. In the back of everyone's mind, including my own, was, *Will the kid be able to pull it off?*

Compounding the pressure was the fact that I'd played the lead character only a few times before, and never had I been asked to carry a *four-hour* film. Relatively few actors in history have even attempted it let alone succeeded at it. Would I be able to maintain an audience's interest for that length of time? I had no idea—all I knew for sure was that I was far out on a limb and shaking like a leaf.

And that's not all. With just moments to go before the camera would roll, I hadn't the slightest idea what to do with the scene, and that is the kind of problem that makes even veteran actors quake in their boots. You see, the scene was tricky for the same reason the audition had been. The script reads like this:

> Woe to you, Korazin! Woe to you, Bethsaida! If the miracles that were performed in you had been performed in Tyre and Sidon, they would have repented long ago in sackcloth and ashes. But I tell you, it will be more bearable for Tyre and Sidon on the day of judgment than for you.
>
> And you, Capernaum, will you be lifted up to the skies? No, you will go down to the depths. If the miracles that were performed in you had been performed in Sodom, it would have remained to this day. But I tell you that it will be more bearable for Sodom on the day of judgment than for you.
>
> (MATTHEW 11:21-24)

Heavy stuff. I'll tell you, as much as I learned Jesus is full of joy and brimming with love, that's how much I learned that you don't go messing with Him. He's as big as it gets, and He's very cut and dried—no gray zone ("You either gather with Me or you scatter"). Psalms says the breath from His nostrils shakes the planet—definitely not someone to mess with.

But that's what presented the difficulty—the words appear so harsh and condemning, yet the hallmark of the Savior giving them was compassion, love, and mercy. How could I fuse the two together for purposes of reenacting the event with any degree of accuracy?

I knew in my *head* that Jesus loved these people and that was key. I had touched on it in the audition. But this was the big leagues—that camera was going to roll in minutes, and it was going to roll right down my throat. Audiences across the world were going to make judgments about Jesus based on what I did in the next half hour, and cast and crew were counting on me to come through. All I could think to do was *pray.*

And pray I did. As hard as I'd prayed before—in preparation, on the journey to Morocco, that morning in the shower—I'd never prayed as hard as I did right then, standing in that Quarzazate marketplace. I was desperate like I'd never known desperate.

113

There were hundreds of bodies milling around me. There were donkeys and camels and children chasing goats; Moroccans sitting along every wall and hanging out every window and doorway; crew racing back and forth with tools and cables; apostles behind me, waiting and small-talking; Regardt working high on a scaffolding alongside the camera. It was a melee of first-century activity mixed with filmmaking technology—and in the middle of it all, I paced along the focus mark F.C. had given me, staring over the crowd and privately praying.

My acting coach, Al Ruscio, used to quote the saying, "The journey from the head to the heart is a journey of a thousand miles." Somehow I knew it was that journey that had to be taken before the cameras rolled, so that was the specific focus of my prayer—a prayer that, for the first time in my life, went like this: "*Lord,* show me what it all looks like through Your eyes."

It's essential for an actor to grasp the character's point of view. The world looks different to different people and therein lies the difference in people's reactions and sensitivities. A good example is two people looking at the same homeless person. One's heart is broken, the other's gets annoyed, resulting in two very different responses.

This "point of view" was something I had yet to tap into with regard to Jesus. I'd never considered it before, but that morning I was begging for it.

And please understand, I wasn't seeking any kind of spiritual experience or vision. I was simply trying to grasp a mindset—*His* mindset—trying to get a handle on what those people looked like to Him 2000 years ago; what we look like to Him today, 2000 years later.

Everyone was swarming around me, paying no attention. I was pacing and praying and looking over the tide of faces, "Lord, show me what it all looks like through Your eyes."

This is where it gets difficult because I don't have words to describe what happened in the next moment.

It was so fast—just a fraction of a fraction of a second—and I'm convinced the reason it was so quick was that the Lord was protecting me. And what I "saw" in that moment was not with my eyes—it was something in my heart. And the only way I can put it into words is to say it was

a sea of people living lives in ways He didn't plan.

People living lives away from His love, away from His care; outside of His goodness, His embrace, His plans, purposes, and hopes for them.

It was so awful a thing—I don't have words to describe to you how incredibly awful it was. I remember when it happened, it was as if the wind got knocked out of me; I couldn't breathe, and my heart just *broke.* It broke on a level I never knew existed, and I just started shaking, and weeping . . . I would weep uncontrollably that day for more than an hour, completely unable to compose my emotions.

And in the pit of all that, as I stood sobbing and shaking, the Lord stamped a Scripture on my heart—and I mean *stamped.* It rose in me like nothing ever has; for lack of any better way to put it, it was as if it actually "came to life" in me. It's a Scripture I'd read a thousand times:

When he saw the crowds, he had compassion on them,
because they were harassed and helpless,
like sheep without a shepherd.

For the first time in my life, I understood what the word "compassion" means when it comes to Jesus Christ. I understood that it isn't just feeling sorry for people; it's a heartbreak so intense, so deep it's like your gut is getting ripped open. It is a heartbreak that screams in utter agony for the needless, pointless pain of people— people who need only turn to Him. What I felt that day was so incredibly tragic. And there can be no doubt what I tasted was just a drop of water in the oceans of the universe compared to what it truly feels like for *Him.* The compassion for people—what it all looks like through His eyes.

Young apostle Matthew, played by dear brother Matthew Roberts, saw it happen. He said by chance he was looking over at me when suddenly he saw my face change dramatically, and then I broke. He told me somehow, instinctively, he sensed what was going on, and stunned to disbelief, he whispered these very scary words to himself: "He's living it."

Matthew's first reaction was to go to me, but Regardt was also watching from the scaffolding. He knew something special was going on, and he wanted to capture it on film. Technically things weren't quite ready, but the moment was already happening so he took a chance and yelled, "Action!"

"Woe to you, Korazin! Woe to you, Bethsaida!" I screamed through trembling lips, with sobbing eyes and a gash in my heart. It was killing me. These people were all going to their death—they were all living in death—and they had no idea; and all they had to do was take His reaching hand. It wasn't, "You heathens are damned!" It was, "Open your eyes! Save yourselves! *Come to Me!*"

It was the desperate scream of a parent watching his own child step off a curb in front of a moving car. If you can imagine that pain, that is what it was. *That's* the heartbreak. *That's* the compassion.

I finished the speech and fell crying into Matthew's arms. There were hundreds out there, but you could hear a pin drop. Regardt cut the scene, and F.C. came down from the camera scaffolding—he was crying himself: "That wasn't acting, brother; that was ministry." Still sobbing, I looked for a place to hide, but there was none. I made my way to a mud wall and sat with my face down, surrounded by villagers. Regardt came—there were tears in his eyes as well. He reached to me, "Are you okay?"

I will never forget looking up into his face and saying, *"It kills Him, Reg. It just kills Him."* It was all I could think to say. Then I broke all over again.

Regardt just hugged me. "I know, I know." Somehow he understood what I was talking about, and I couldn't help but sense in his grip and tone a stirring of righteous anger. He continued, "That's why we're out here, brother. That's why we're doing what we're doing."

Set photographer Robby Botha, the pro that he is, had his eyes on me when the whole thing happened. He whipped his camera off his shoulder and sprang into action, leveling a long lens from across the marketplace, capturing it all with the aid of a speed shutter. Two months later I was shown that strip of negatives and I lost it all over

117

again, the memory flooding back. Where my words have fallen so short of conveying the whole thing, Robby's photos say it all.

Then, bad news came down from the scaffolding. There were focus problems—we would have to do another take. It took the breath out of Regardt to tell me that, but what could he do? Heartbreakingly, what had happened would be lost to all but those of us who were there.

To this day I've never seen that piece of film, though Reg has. Every time it's mentioned, he gets very serious—"It's something amazing, my 'Bru.' You wouldn't believe your eyes if you saw it. I tried every way I could, but it just wasn't usable." The sense of loss when he talks about it is overwhelming.

Eventually we were ready to try a second take. I was still very broken, so it looked like we might duplicate the first. The camera rolled, and I began in the same experience of pain. But out of nowhere, a very comical thing happened. The first "Woe" was barely out when a few feet away, a sheep bleated as loud as a sheep can bleat, *"B-a-a-a-a-h-h-h!"* It was so loud, so intrusive, and so perfectly timed—it was comic genius. All my tension released in laughter, snapping the mood like a dry twig.

The camera continued to roll, however, so the speech rolled as well, to the very end. Being behind schedule, we were forced to print that take and go with it. Unfortunately, in the final edit my sheep friend got filtered out of the soundtrack, and his bid for stardom went with it (serves him right for stealing the scene).

In any event, the shot was in the can, and the experience was ingrained in all our hearts. As remarkable as it was, there was work still to be done that day, so we did the only thing we could do—we moved on to the next scene, the next adventure, the next challenge, the next glory. How much deeper could it possibly get—and it was only Day 2?

A funny thing about that "Woe to Korazin" scene—it was a huge scene, and normally big scenes like that are scheduled well into a shoot to give the cast and crew time to warm into their respective roles. Some would say it was a blunder to schedule a scene that big so early. But as I see it in retrospect, it was no blunder at all—*it was God*. He needed me to experience that scene—that heartache, that compassion—right off the bat. He needed me to understand His heart like

119

that right away, and for it to be etched in my heart from the very beginning so it would come through everything I did in front of that camera: "Come to Me! Come to Me! Come to Me!" That's what He needed the people to see; that's what He needed the people to know; that's what He needed *Matthew* to be—*Come to Me!*

———————

The rest of Day 2 is mostly a blur. I remember being unhappy about some of my work in other scenes and being exhausted all through the afternoon. I don't remember what the conversation was in the hammam that night, or even at supper, or even if I had supper. I do remember that everyone was feeling bad about losing that first take.

I've tossed and turned many hours over that myself, with little satisfaction. It's just one of those unexplainable things where all a guy can do is rest in the Lord and trust His sovereignty over the situation. Maybe it was something the Lord just wanted for those of us who were out there. Maybe it was something just for the Moroccans to see. Maybe it was something going on in the spiritual realm that we'll only learn about in heaven. All one can do is trust Him in it and move on.

A summer ago, over lunch, I would tell this story to a dear friend, actor Dean Jones. I asked him what one does with a thing like that yanking on his emotions, screaming for expression. In Dean's marvelous wisdom, he calmly replied, "You must do as Scripture says Mary did with all the wonders she witnessed in her Son—she 'pondered all these things in her heart.'"

And so I do. But you know, there's a flip-side to this whole story, to the heartbreak and compassion. It occurred to me just recently as I watched over a hundred newly saved brothers and sisters go through the waters of baptism in a church service. It was a stunning sight— folks of every race, color, size, shape, background; men, women, young, not-so-young—all before Jesus. It hit me that as devastating as the heartbreak of Jesus is over the multitude of lives living in ways He didn't plan, as much as it tears His heart to shreds—that's how excited He is when even *one* of those lives comes home to Him. One of His babies reaching up to take His outstretched hand and fall into

His waiting embrace—it's undoubtedly the most beautiful sight in all the world to His smiling eyes. It is unquestionably His fullest moment—the moment He lives and longs for—the moment He died for—*Come to Me!*

> Come to me, all you who are weary and burdened,
> and I will give you rest. . . .
> Learn from me,
> for I am gentle and humble in heart,
> and you will find rest for your souls.
>
> *Jesus*

DIRTY FEET AND ROUGH BUT GENTLE HANDS

CHAPTER EIGHT

. . . taking the very nature of a servant. . . .

PHILIPPIANS 2:7

ROPPED ON A SHELF IN MY LIVING ROOM sits a water-color portrait of Jesus given me by one of *Matthew*'s crowd extras. Just to its right is the crown of thorns I wore during the crucifixion scenes, and an 8 x 4 x 4-inch rectangular, rust-colored rock. I love to watch people when they visit for the first time. They inevitably go straight to the crown of thorns (it's quite a thing to behold), then to the watercolor, and finally back to the thorns for a last open-mouthed peek—all the while ignoring that rust-colored rock.

I've never asked, but I can only guess everyone passes by that rock assuming it's nothing more than a tasteless attempt at interior deco-rating. But truth be told, that rock is no interior decoration at all. That rock, in fact, was specifically selected from a cornfield just off the Ventura Highway in Encino, California. And believe it or not, it played an integral role in our presentation of Jesus in *Matthew*.

Flashback to December 8, 1992—that now-familiar Los Angeles lunch meeting with Regardt. One of the things we discussed that afternoon was the physicality of Jesus—what He would have looked like. Regardt felt strongly that Jesus was not the soft, thin, cream-skinned, manicured figure He is traditionally pictured to be. In truth, Reg felt Jesus was very much the opposite—that He was very *real*, and very *physical*. That reality, that physicality, Regardt felt compelled to bring to the screen—possibly for the first time in film history.

I'll never forget standing in the hotel lobby that day, as Reg and I were about to part ways. He had that patented sparkle in his eyes and matching excitement in his voice (I could see he could hardly wait to grab a camera and yell, "Action!"). He leaned in close and got very intense and described the arms of Jesus, drawing his own arm taut in a fisted clench to drive the point: "Dark forearms rippling with muscle and veins as His hands move. Not like a bodybuilder, but arms that know hard work and heavy labor."

Of course! Jesus was no spoiled kid raised on satin pillows. His earthly father was a blue-collar worker, a laborer—a carpenter by trade. He was a man who worked *with his hands*, earning a living by the sweat of his brow. And as his firstborn son, Jesus would necessarily have followed suit, starting from that first day He was old enough to lift a nail and carry it across the room to Dad's workbench.

Keep in mind that this is a *first-century* carpenter. We're not talking power tools and prefab moldings—we're talking seriously heavy work with seriously crude tools. There wasn't anything soft or manicured about it. It was rugged, gut-it-out, sweat-and-sawdust manual labor.

It's a picture of Jesus we seldom think about: perspiring in the sun from dawn to dusk, hoisting timbers, carving, shaping, sawing, sanding. Panting in the afternoon heat, hair matted with dirt and dust and workshop grime. Working endless hours into the night, pushing to meet deadlines over the days, weeks, years. Singing psalms at the top of His lungs while planing doors, carving plows, and fitting ox yokes.

Make no mistake about it, Jesus knew what it was to get His hands dirty. He knew the meaning of hard work. It's undoubtedly how He spent most of His earthly life; and over the course of those hours, days, weeks, months, and years, Jesus would necessarily have developed those powerful arms Regardt so intensely described that cold December day in Los Angeles.

And along with them, Jesus would have developed a serious set of shoulders, an iron chest, rock-solid legs. And picture His hands—thick and dark, broad and calloused, strong and experienced, dirt under the fingernails, scarred and bruised from years of scrapes, blisters, splinters, and strain. Given the physical demands of His life, I can't imagine how it could have been otherwise.

Jesus' physicality—His strength, His brawn, His power—really hit home to me when I was studying the crucifixion. It's a strange thing about the crucifixion, there's a part of us that doesn't want to deal with the physical realities of what actually happened to Jesus that day. As we love and adore Him, it isn't very pleasant to consider the base details of His pain and the cold facts of His suffering. But you see, I was forced to deal with them for purposes of the work that lay in front of me. I was forced to tear away the blinders and stare down the ugly throat of it, and, as you can imagine, I was dragged into some pretty eye-opening discoveries.

One of those discoveries had to do with the Roman flogging Jesus suffered at the hands of Pontius Pilate. I was shocked to learn most prisoners didn't even survive it. Most guys would die right there, as their bodies were flayed open by the metal, bone, and rock laced through the leather thongs. And of the handful who did survive, most would seize in shock and go mad or comatose as their systems shut down against the onslaught of pain and violation.

Now, it's a huge mistake to think, *well, Jesus was the Son of God, so of course He would make it through with shining colors.* Yes, He was the Son of God, but He was 100-percent human as well, and His body would have reacted to those horrors no differently from yours or mine. And we're not just talking about a whipping—He endured two mob beatings and the torture of those thorns as well.

But you see (and I so love this), Jesus was fully conditioned for His mission—spiritually, emotionally, intellectually, *and* physically. Do you realize how fit, how tough, how stalwart, how powerful His body must have been to take that mountain of assault and still have the grit to tackle Golgotha—to still have the might in His legs to climb that hill and the force in His arms to pull against those nails for *hours* before finally, inevitably giving out?

Did you ever wonder, *Why a carpenter? Why not some more prestigious profession, something more befitting the Son of the Living God?* In view of the physical demands of the cross, I can't help but marvel at how those years as a carpenter would have served so perfectly to condition Jesus for every step of it. I mean, the Father knew His Son would need a serious measure of strength and endurance to fulfill His mission, and what better way to build that in Him than 20-plus years of heavy labor!

Amazing thought, isn't it? It screams of the Father's attention to detail, the subtlety with which He works, and the totality with which He equips and provides. I'm not saying the sole reason Jesus was a carpenter was so He could handle the cross—I'd be a fool to speak for the Father's motivations like that. But it's hard to ignore the way it weaves in so nicely. And I can't help but think it's something of a pattern for the way the Father works in all our lives when we're honestly seeking and welcoming His purposes: He tiptoes behind the scenes, quietly preparing us, giving us exactly what we need, all the while taking us down paths that seem so mundane—maybe even foolish.

Think about it: What could be more mundane—more foolish—than the Son of God spending His time sawing wood and hammering nails? When you step back and look at it, it's shocking! But Scripture tells us the wisdom of God seems foolish to men (1 Corinthians 2:14). His ways are *definitely* not our ways—even when it comes to His own Son! So when life seems to be nothing but "sawing wood and hammering nails," think of Jesus and buckle your seatbelt.

But back to His physicality (and here's where that rust-colored rock ties in), when Regardt and I first talked, I wasn't exactly a pale little wimp. I'd always been pretty athletic, and as an actor, keeping in shape was part of my job. But in spite of that, I wasn't even close to making any kind of a realistic Jesus statement, so as I drove away from the hotel that day, I found myself with a lot of beefing up and a little slimming down to do—and just seven weeks to do it in.

Time was against me, but that wasn't the biggest challenge. What concerned me most was I had no equipment, no gym membership, and too little cash flow to do anything about either. How was I going to get serious arms and shoulders in seven weeks with nothing but rain and smog to train with? Have no fear! Never let it be said that I'm not a resourceful person.

I remembered a small cornfield (you guessed it) just off the Ventura Highway in Encino, whose winding dirt paths used to provide my favorite running course. I couldn't take my eyes off the ground as I ran those paths because there were rocks strewn all over them—rocks that were the ideal size and shape for a makeshift dumbbell—exactly what I needed to develop those arms Regardt talked about. It was the best idea I could come up with, so I jumped in my pickup and drove to that cornfield in search of the perfect workout rock. It had to be weighty enough to do damage, somewhat balanced, and thin enough to fit into my grip.

Sounds hilarious, doesn't it? Though at the time it wasn't very nice to have to resort to such things, looking back, I wouldn't have had it any other way. I mean, sure, I could have whipped out the credit card and bought a membership to the finest Gym to the Stars that Beverly Hills had to offer, but how smart would it have been to build debt like that? And besides, as bizarre as it may sound, there was something so "right" about it being rocks and cornfields. Don't ask me to explain why, but it's just the way it needed to be.

Anyway, I walked the muddy paths of that cornfield with the winter sun sinking behind the surrounding hills, looking high and low for the perfect rock. This one was too light, this one was too fat, this one didn't have the right balance. . . . Finally, with just a glimmer of light remaining and the wind blasting cold through my shirt sleeves—voilà! There it was, resting against the base of a dirt mound—that 8 x 4 x 4-inch rectangular, rust-colored rock that sits on my shelf to this day.

I knew it was the right rock the second I laid eyes on it. I knocked the dirt away, wrapped a hand around it, did a couple test curls, smiled big, and thanked God for His faithfulness—He'd provided exactly what I needed. Within minutes I was back on the road, rushing home for that first Fred Flintstone workout. Hallelujah!

My daily routine was simple, and I pounded it out religiously (no pun intended)—a four-mile run with my dog, situps, leg lifts, pushups, and finally, arms and shoulders with the rock. I'd take it in my right hand and curl until I couldn't lift it one more time, then switch to the left and do the same back and forth, over and over. Then it was time for triceps, forearms, wrists—rep after rep, set after set, until every imaginable tissue was cramped. And here's the funny part—all the while I recited the Sermon on the Mount, or a parable, or whatever other passage I happened to be memorizing that day. It must have been a hilarious sight. My dog would just lie on the floor licking his paws and staring up at me as if to say, "I'm not so sure I'm completely getting this, Dad."

It was funny, that's for sure, but I also remember it as a terribly lonely time as well. I can still hear the rain drumming off my brick patio and the radio playing softly as I stood alone, night after night, facing the closet mirror with that rust-colored rock—up and down, up and down, up and down. . . . *Blessed are the poor in spirit, for theirs is the kingdom of heaven. Blessed are those who mourn, for they will be comforted. Blessed are the meek.* . . . My fingers and wrists would seize up, time after time, night after night. Most of those nights, the minutes felt like hours.

But it worked. That first evening in the Quarzazate hammam, Regardt looked at me through the steam and said, "You did a lot of work on your body, didn't you? I can see it. *It looks right.*" That comment made it worth every cramped muscle, every dry baked potato dinner, every run through piercing rain, every lonely hour of every lonely night pumping that little rock every which way—I'd do it all again in a heartbeat! Praise God for the grace He gave me to push through those seven weeks.

One of the biggest blessings of the *Matthew* adventure has flowed directly out of it. Since the film was released, I've had the humbling privilege of seeing legions of young people—junior high and high school—turning on to Jesus for the first time, their attention arrested not only by the joy and passion they never knew was in Him, but also by His *physicality.* I know it seems like an odd reason for someone to turn toward Jesus, but I've discovered that most young people have somehow gotten that soft, porcelain-doll image ingrained in their imaginations. And needless to say, it's an image they don't exactly aspire or look up to. In a sea of role models like Michael Jordan and Jean-Claude van Damme, a delicate, rosy-cheeked figure who looks more like he grew up getting manicures than banging it out on a football field doesn't hold much of a chance.

I love the looks on those kids' faces when that misconception gets blown sky-high and they're confronted with what Jesus was *really* like. Especially when it's those oh-so-cool teenagers—I love to see that "unaffected" half-smile and that head-cocked-to-one-side nod as the thought rumbles behind their eyes, *Wow—I never knew that. This Jesus-dude's okay*—the Lord using the spark of His physicality to light a bonfire of His truth.

And it isn't just Jesus' physicality that strikes people but also who He was within that physicality. It's one thing to be strong, but it's another thing entirely to *live* strong.

Shortly after completing *Matthew,* I was watching one of those beautiful old Jesus movies that comes on television every Easter. I

129

remember in particular a transitional scene where Jesus and the apostles were together in a boat, shoving off from the Galilean shoreline. The Twelve were working like dogs to get the vessel going—hoisting sails, securing rigging, straining, paddling—all against a tremendous headwind. But with all this going on, Jesus sat silent and alone, regally poised in the stern, hypnotically staring into the far reaches of the blue horizon—much too important, much too preoccupied, off in a world of His own.

Now, forgive me if I sound a bit critical or even disrespectful—I really don't mean to. Everyone has their own interpretation, and I can't say that I'm right and everyone else is wrong. But if the Jesus I discovered has any validity whatsoever, He would no sooner have sat there with everyone working around Him than He would have ridden a limousine into Jerusalem instead of a donkey. The Jesus I discovered would be right in there with those guys, getting His hands dirty, working and sweating with the best of them. He'd be pushing and pulling, yanking and straining, lifting and hoisting, and loving every second of it. He'd be grinning from ear to ear, enjoying the astounding machinery of His own human body and the breathtaking dynamics of His marvelous creation—the sea, the wind, the waves, the sunset.

He'd be having great fun with His pals, belting out at the top of His lungs, "Keep it coming, boys! We've almost got it! Praise You, glorious Father—You're mighty and magnificent, indeed!" Bigger than life itself, beyond robust, brimming with all the excitement and vitality that life can offer—every bit a *man*, in the true sense of the word, living life to its fullest every precious second of every precious day. If we could grasp just one fraction of the "bigness," the champion, the absolute *roar* that He was 2000 years ago. Jesus wasn't called "the pussycat of Judah"—He was called "the *Lion* of Judah" and believe me, He wasn't called that for nothing. Hallelujah!

Now it's time for me to brag a bit. I give all the glory to God for everything that happened on *Matthew*—all that got on film and every incredible blessing that's flowed from it since. But there is one thing I am very proud of, and it's the only thing I feel free to boast about. You know all the other Jesus movies? They're all blessings in their own right, and lives have been transformed through every one. But

I'm beyond thrilled to proclaim to the world that (drum roll and fanfare, please) . . .

I'm the only "Jesus" in film history
whose hair moves when the wind blows.

Come on, now! Don't be laughing at me! It's true. Watch any other Jesus movie and you'll see it as plain as day—the wind is whipping furiously, the Sea of Galilee is an uproar, palm trees are bobbing and weaving, but Jesus' hair somehow stays perfectly combed! Maybe it's a miracle the Gospel writers never recorded, or maybe they used hairspray in the first century—I don't know. All I know is on our film set, when the wind blew, my hair was flying! And if you'll pardon me, I'm proud of it!

All silliness aside, it actually brings up a nugget of truth that's important to grab hold of. Jesus lived a specific lifestyle giving rise to a specific reality, and He must have chosen that lifestyle—that reality—for a specific reason. There must be something He's trying to tell us through it—something about Himself and who He is as God. I mean, He chose to be born into a feed trough in a barn in the middle of nowhere; that's not very glamourous when you step back and take a hard look at it. He could have chosen Herod's palace or Caesar's throne room or any number of splendid birthplaces—but He didn't. He chose—and this is so vital to grasp—the complete *opposite of splendor*, the ugliest and *lowliest* of birthplaces.

I know we've prettied up the whole thing with poetic words and glittering nativity scenes, but that's simply not the way it was 2000 years ago. For Mary's sake alone, I wish it had been even half that lovely in reality—but it wasn't. And as well-meaning as it may be when we romanticize and (forgive me) "religionize" that reality away, we romanticize away *His* reality as well, painting over that very specific something about His nature that He's trying so desperately to tell us through it.

Think about it—as wonderful as all the painters and lyricists and orators may be, who could possibly paint a better picture of Jesus than He painted for Himself, in all its lackluster. Yes, when you really step back and look at it, the picture Jesus painted for Himself—the life He chose to live—was anything but pretty in any way, shape, or form.

131

Remember the story I told you about the feeding of the 5000—the sweat, the dust, the wind, the humanity? My robes were so far from clean, it wasn't funny. Dirt and perspiration stained every crease and fold. My face was dark and weathered by sun and wind, my feet were caked and scraped and aching with fatigue. And for me it was only 12 hours or so—for Jesus it was all day, every day. Fishing boats, country roads, campfires, dirt floors—these were the day-in, day-out physical realities Jesus lived.

Now that I think about it, maybe that was one of the stumbling blocks for the Pharisees. They had painted for themselves a picture of Messiah that Jesus didn't exactly match up to. They were looking for silken robes, shimmering chariots, and a flashing sword. That's who they wanted their beloved Messiah to be—and that's probably a big reason they wanted nothing to do with who He truly was.

The funny thing is, if anyone should have recognized Him, it was those guys. Their whole lives were about God and awaiting Messiah. They "dressed" God, they "talked" God, they even "ate" God. They knew the Messianic prophecies backward and forward, and it was so blatantly obvious—"Behold, your King is coming to you, *lowly,* and sitting on a donkey." But in spite of the glaring truth, they insisted on *their* idea of a king—dare I say, maybe even *our* idea of a king. Then in walks Jesus, who blows everyone's mind with *His* idea of a king:

> *Whoever wants to become great among you must be your servant;*
> *and whoever wants to be first must be your slave.*

Jesus—the son of a peasant girl and a laborer. Jesus—a man who didn't even have a home to call His own. Jesus—who hung out with prostitutes, thieves, cripples, and even a few fishermen. Jesus—a man who was more interested in matters of the heart than anything else. Jesus—a seemingly common, young, small-town man: sleeves rolled up, hair tossed and tumbled by a gust of first-century wind, face tanned and weathered, rough and calloused hands, dirt under the fingernails, soiled feet in well-worn sandals.

Jesus—sweat glistening on the brow, creases framing gentle eyes— eyes that look deep into your soul and inescapably breathe "I love you" with every glance. And a smile—oh, what a smile—as big as the sun, beaming at you and you alone as if you're the only person on the entire planet. *Jesus.*

Shortly after we finished filming, I was speaking in a Cape Town church on a beautiful summer Sunday evening. Early in the service, the pastor's teenage daughter walked up to the platform with two friends and announced they had prepared a song for me. She said she'd been on the set a month or so before, working as one of the multitude in the feeding of the 5000. She said, "As I watched you playing Jesus out there, I kept thinking of this song because it's what I saw happening."

I relaxed in my chair, anticipating nothing more than a cute blessing. I had another thing coming. When those girls began to harmonize a cappella, a sweet presence of the Lord filled the room like few times

I'd ever experienced, and it was grab-a-tissue-and-hold-on-for-dear-life time.

The song they sang was one I'd heard for the first time just a couple weeks before. The actor who played young apostle Matthew gave it to me on tape, saying the exact same thing this girl had. I remember plugging that tape into my player and lying on my hotel bed for a quick listen before turning the lights out. My eyes were heavy and my mind fixed on sleep, but when that song began to play—wow. I played it over and over for a good hour, hanging on every lyric. The song was about Jesus, and it spoke exactly what I was feeling in the role, confirming what I knew in my heart to be right, but what I also knew was such a risk. As I listened, it was as if the Lord Himself was saying through those headphones, "You're doing good, kid. You just keep on going. Don't be tired, don't be afraid—just keep on going."

I would listen to that song many times a day in the coming weeks for encouragement and grounding. But as many times as I'd heard it, I never heard it like I heard it that Sunday night in that Cape Town church out of the mouths of those three amateur teenage girls. The purity, the simplicity, the innocence, the humility—it just was more than I could handle.

It's a song I'm sure many of you know. It was written by Michael Card, and it goes like this:

> The Gentle Healer came into our town today;
> He touched blind eyes and the darkness left to stay.
> But more than the blindness, He took their sins away;
> The Gentle Healer came into our town today.
>
> The Gentle Healer came into our town today;
> He spoke one word, that was all He had to say;
> And the one who had died just rose up straight away.
> The Gentle Healer came into our town today.
>
> Oh, He seems like just an ordinary man,
> With *dirty feet and rough but gentle hands.*
> But the words He says are hard to understand;
> And yet He seems like just an ordinary man.
>
> The Gentle Healer, He left our town today;
> I just looked around and found He'd gone away.

Some folks from town who've followed Him, they say,
That the Gentle Healer is the Truth, the Life, the Way.*

The Gentle Healer—for my money, the consummate Jesus song. *Ordinary man . . . the Way, the Truth, the Life . . . dirty feet and rough but gentle hands.*

Jesus!

---

* *The Gentle Healer* © 1986 Birdwing Music (ASCAP)/Mole End Music Adm. by EMI Christian Music Publishing. All rights reserved. Used by permission.

WHAT A GUY!

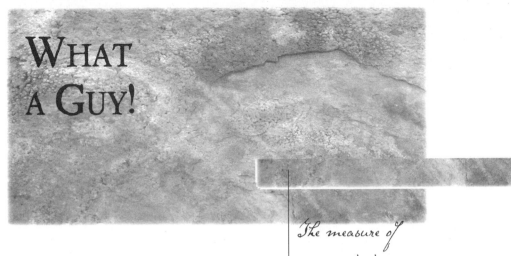

CHAPTER NINE

The measure of a man is in his actions.

$\mathcal{I}$ JUST HAVE TO SHARE another story that involves yet again the day-to-day realities of Jesus' life. I know, "We've talked that into the ground, Bruce." But before you shout a hearty amen, give me a chance to explain.

First, you must understand, those realities are at the core of the film and all that was learned. Out of them flowed *everything*—I just can't stress this enough.

Second, by way of confession, I have this tendency to repeat myself (as if you haven't noticed). But it's only when I'm passionate about something, and this Jesus rises in me like nothing ever has: His vitality, His intimacy, His excitement, His heroism—wow!

Here's the story. . .

A few years ago I sat in a South African prison chapel, waiting for a *Matthew* film clip to finish before I addressed the inmates. It was Victor Verster Prison, one of the two prisons where Nelson Mandela was housed following his Robin Island years. At that point, prisons were a whole new ballgame to me, and I was somewhat intimidated. There was no threat from the prisoners themselves, but my life experience was so vastly removed from theirs I couldn't imagine how I could possibly relate to them.

There was only one hope, and I knew it—pray! So there I sat, silently begging the Lord to give me something to say to these men. "Lord, what can I say to these guys? I don't know them!" I will never forget the response that rose in my heart.

> You don't need to know them, Bruce—*I* know them.
> I know every name, every struggle, every hurt,
> every hope, every dream. . . .
> I know them.

I'm not sure how that strikes anyone else, but for me, that's as profound as it gets—*He knows.* I told the prisoners that, and we all sat there for a few minutes, dumbfounded. When raw truth hits, there's not much anyone can say. Eventually, though, I went on to talk of things that had never before occurred to me. It went something like this:

> You think you had it rough as a kid? This Guy was born in a barn. His first bed was a feed trough. He wasn't even two years old and people were trying to kill Him. He had to hide out with His mom and dad—on the run, and just a baby. And that went on His entire life. Folks were always plotting to kill Him—eventually they did.
>
> Did you grow up being laughed at and kicked around? Imagine Jesus hearing the laughs about His mom being pregnant before she was married, getting teased and spit at by other kids because of it.
>
> Did you grow up without a father or mother? Divorce, death, or maybe one just walked out on you? You know, Joseph is never mentioned after Jesus is 12. Nobody knows for sure what happened to him, but most experts figure he must have died when Jesus was just a kid. Yeah, guys, Jesus knows that heartbreak. Imagine Him standing at His dad's grave. And as the eldest son, He'd have to carry on and support the family. See Him in His dad's workshop that first day, reaching for His father's tools, tears streaming down His face—and just a kid.
>
> Ever had no place to sleep? "Foxes have holes and birds of the air have nests, but the Son of Man has no place to lay his head"—the words of Jesus. He even knows what it's like to have no place to live—sleeping around campfires or on people's floors.

Ever had anyone beat your face in? You guessed it—the Bible says they beat Jesus so badly you couldn't even tell He was a human being.

Friends run out on you? Jesus had a couple choice buddies named Judas and Peter.

And He even knows what it's like to be in a place like this. He knows because they locked Him up once.

Yeah, *Jesus knows*, guys. He knows *every* struggle, *every* heartache. And not just because He's God and God knows everything; but because when He was a man, He went through the same things you and I go through and more. He knows because He lived it. *He's been there.*

That's the story as best as I can remember, and the reason I've added it is because I've seen it mean a lot to folks over the past couple years of telling it. It's an incredible proposition when you stop to think about it. With all that's going on, no matter who you are or what it may be: *He knows.*

"What a Guy!" It's a phrase I've used more times than I can count. Please know that I mean it with all the reverence and honor in the world, and not just because Jesus is God and that commands serious respect. All deity aside, this Jesus was a Man such as never walked the planet before or since, a Man of such mountainous character, such mind-blowing integrity, such breathtaking heroism, there just are no words to do Him justice. So, in my unpoetic manner, all I can come up with to say is, "What a Guy!"

Remember that acting lesson I mentioned—"The measure of a man is in his *actions*; in what he *does*"? When it came to Jesus, the more I explored His "what He does"—*wow!*

Consistently, He spoke truth against a sea of opposition. Shockingly, He lived fully in His personal life exactly what He preached in public. Time after time, He stood heroically alone for what was right, regardless of what it might cost Him. Without hesitation, He went out of His way to care for the most objectionable people of society, never turning a hungry soul away, always taking time to love an unlovable or care for an uncareable, knowing He would suffer ridicule and rejection for it. Humbly and openly, He marched across cultural barriers, decrying centuries of racist arrogance. Never a respecter of persons, unconcerned with status, wealth, gender, or popularity, He

139

stood, champion and friend of the "little guy." And for all this and more, He constantly took it on the chin, keeping His mouth shut, His face set like flint, eyes riveted on His greater cause and mission.

You know, we picture Jesus in the face of the Pharisees' accusations, standing calmly in ethereal peace. But do you really think it was easy for Him to be openly insulted and lied about like that, and by people who meant the world to Him? These were people He longed to gather "as a hen gathers her chicks under her wings"—people who were His very own kids.

All He wanted was to care for them, protect them, save them, love them; and all they could do was spit in His face. Put yourself in His shoes—can there be anything more grieving than having your own kids spit in your face? It was His usual lot, and it must have torn His heart to shreds.

Anyway, this was truly a Man among men, bigger than life itself yet as down-to-earth as it gets. This was the ultimate definition of masculinity, the very personification of character and integrity. He was the human coming-together of everything that is truly noble, good, honorable, and magnificent. Jesus!

We all go crazy for the big-screen hero—the guy who storms in against all odds, giving all to rescue some helpless (and coincidentally gorgeous) waif. We've all seen van Damme or Stallone, bulging muscles in torn T-shirts, toting a twenty-third-century megaweapon with which 53 people will be mowed down before the opening credits pass.

But take a look at Jesus—a solitary figure, bruised and bleeding—the sword of Truth His only weapon. Picture Him raising it again and again, fighting an army of world attitudes: "Lie, cheat—anything goes!" "He who dies with the most toys wins!" Picture Him storming in against overwhelming opposition, giving His literal all—*His very life*—to rescue the helpless, the widowed, the orphaned, the crushed, the rejected, the despised. I don't know about you, but in my book, that's the living definition of "hero"—the *true* definition of hero.

SCENE 211—JERUSALEM TEMPLE—DAY EXTERIOR
The violence of a table being overturned into the camera.
The enraged JESUS steps over the table and overturns
another. MONEY LENDERS scatter. We follow JESUS on
His path of destruction.

It was another one of those scenes that made me uncomfortable. As I approached it that morning in Cape Town, something wasn't making sense, as Jesus' behavior again seemed outside of His loving character. I mean, to throw a tantrum because people were offending His Father? People were *constantly* offending His Father; it was His daily diet—why respond so explosively on this particular occasion?

I remember pulling Regardt aside and asking why Jesus needed to be angry in the scene. I asked specifically, "Is it scriptural, Reg, or are we just accustomed to picturing it that way?" Reg called in Bruce Rudnick with his tattered Bible, and we three sat on the "temple" steps with the crew working around us to talk it through.

Our meeting proved unfruitful. We decided that indeed, Jesus would be angry when the cameras rolled—*but why?* That's what I couldn't seem to get to. Finally, with the guys tending to last-minute details, I reached into my backpack, cracked open my research notes, and voilà! There it was in my own handwriting from three months earlier—a golden discovery unlocking the entire mystery, fitting everything together perfectly, and painting a picture of Jesus even more loving and more heroic than I'd experienced before that day.

Yes, Jesus was "consumed with zeal" for His Father's house—no doubt about it. He was an unhappy Messiah about the big business they'd turned His Father into. But there was more going on there than immediately strikes the eye. It was Passover—festival time—and tens of thousands were pouring into Jerusalem from all over the ancient world to offer their sacrifices in worship, as required by the Law. But what specifically did the Law require? That's where the temple leaders came in—it was their job to interpret and administrate that Law—to instruct the masses on what was acceptable as a sacrifice and what was not.

For all practical purposes, the requirements these fellows came up with were next to impossible to meet: "A white male lamb, under a year old, born on a rainy day between October and December, raised on cornmeal and Bermuda grass stems." Of course I'm exaggerating to make the point, but from what I could gather, their specifications weren't much more realistic. And here's the catch: by and large, the people were incredibly poor. Most couldn't even afford to own one of these animals, let alone tow it to Jerusalem just to have it slaughtered behind closed doors. Jesus sure wasn't lying when He said about these leaders, "They tie up heavy loads and put them on men's shoulders."

But not making a sacrifice at Passover wasn't an option. And that's where these guys had the Jewish people between a rock and a hard place. The people were required to bring an impossible-to-find animal for sacrifice, and it just so happened those temple leaders had those animals for sale, *right on the temple steps*. What a surprise. And of course, demand is high with Passover, and we all know what that does to prices. . . .

It doesn't stop there. You know those moneychangers? Folks were coming from every nation, and that meant different currencies— "I'm sorry, we only take Jerusalem dollars; but my cousin Hank, there, will exchange for you." Of course Hank charges through the nose and kicks back to his cousin, and on it goes.

And though I'll probably get booed for this, I've got to say it. I can picture every one of those guys merrily proclaiming, "Look how the Lord is blessing us, brothers! Hallelujah!" But the truth is the truth—

they'd created self-serving systems, gouging the people, justifying it in the name of God, and all the while kicking Him and His children square in the face.

Can you grasp the tragedy that was taking place? Look at the typical first-century Judean who's worked all year, barely scraping a living for his family. He goes to the temple for worship, but all he finds are hawkers screaming above the pushing and shoving thousands. Animal supply is dwindling and prices are climbing, but what can he do—he must make an acceptable sacrifice, so he joins the melee. Running to get currency, he returns with 60 cents on the dollar and shops for something reasonable—it's not to be found. It crosses his mind to just go home—the kids need clothes and the harvest wasn't good this year—but it's the Law, and God's representatives say his sheep aren't good enough, so he pushes a fist of precious cash across the table. It steals his breath to watch it disappear, but what can he do? It's the Law.

That kind of scene was taking place by the thousands, year after year—the "little people" being squeezed, and the temple leaders laughing all the way to the bank. I can only wonder how many times Jesus, as a child, watched His own dad struggle through it. I can only wonder at how many feasts Jesus restrained Himself from exploding as He did at this one. I can see Him standing quietly amid the throngs, calming Himself under His breath, "It's not time yet."

His people were cut off from freely worshiping as He longed for them to by the very men His Father had appointed to facilitate that worship. His children were being manipulated *by the very men His Father had chosen to care for and protect them.* No wonder Jesus was so angry.

Can you imagine watching your own kids kicked around like that? Can you imagine how you'd react? And why? Because you love them.

Yes, the golden discovery: *He loved them.* Therein was the heart of His anger—the compound layers of offense and violation heaped upon His Father and thrust upon His children—*the two He loved the most*—must have pierced Jesus to the very core. And His reaction was *thunder!*

When the Father said, "Now!" Jerusalem must have heard nothing less than thunder. Jesus unloaded on those guys with a wrath they'd only read about in the Prophets and couldn't imagine in real life. And when the dust settled, I bet you could hear a piece of straw hit the ground on the Mount of Olives. And there's Jesus standing in the middle of them, fire in His eyes, red-faced and out of breath, voice coarse with rage, "My house will be called a house of *prayer!*"

Then there are the Twelve. I can see them all in a row, mouths agape, each thinking the exact same thing: *This is it; we're gonna die, right here and now.*

And that's the point—there was a cost to what Jesus did that day, and He was fully aware of it. He knew He was fueling the fires of His own murder. He knew within the hour those temple leaders would be huddling behind closed doors, "He must be eliminated—*now!*" But what's right is right, and somebody has to stand up for it even if it means standing alone. Somebody needs to shout, "Enough is enough, here!" no matter the consequences. And Jesus was that kind of somebody—a figure of towering manhood, standing for the people, standing for the Father—standing alone.

I'm sure there were well-meaning friends that day who pulled Him aside and advised, "You're much too idealistic, you know. Don't be so heavenly minded that you're no earthly good. Besides, that's life—the rich get richer and the poor get poorer. *What are you going to do, change the world?*"

I can see Jesus, smiling from ear to ear, grabbing their faces in His hands, laying a great big kiss on each of them and laughing, "Hallelujah! You're finally getting it! Yes, that's exactly what I'm going to do— *change the world!*" And praise God—He did!

The day we shot that scene was one of the most exciting of the entire shoot. There was great anticipation, as the art department had created every detail of temple authenticity: doves, goats, donkeys, and sheep; produce, pottery, and piles of coins; hawkers, prostitutes, Pharisees, and worshipers. The courtyard of the University of Cape Town was magnificently transformed into first-century reality, and you could feel the electricity of big-scene moviemaking crackling through the air.

Regardt walked me through the sequence: Jesus and the Twelve come up the steps and take in the hubbub. Jesus approaches a table surrounded by moneychangers, pauses, then explodes, continuing through the courtyard. He turns to the Pharisees, speaks His mind, and walks off.

I remember thinking the scene would be a great opportunity to showcase the physical strength of Jesus as well. The tables were heavy, and I wanted to flip them hard, end over end—it would make for great visuals with the coins and all splattering every which way.

Eventually everything was ready to go. It got quiet, the cameras rolled, and Regardt called, "Action!" I'll never forget walking up those steps and seeing all that moneymaking going on and hearing the hawkers yelling. I stood at the first table, looking on piles of shimmering silver, cleared everyone out of harm's way, then *erupted*—and I'm telling you, I went absolutely *nuts!* What took the art department an entire day to construct I destroyed in seconds. When that final table clattered to the ground, every Pharisee, apostle, extra, and crew member was frozen solid. I guess they weren't quite expecting what they got—but then, neither was I. Lying in my hotel bed that night, I knew we'd captured something special on film; and sure enough, to this day it's one of those scenes most everyone wants to know about.

That same "What a Guy" appears over and over in everything Jesus says and does. Think of His healing the man with the shriveled hand on the Sabbath. Healing on that day was a huge offense to the Pharisees, and make no mistake, Jesus knew this. Just as on the temple steps, He knew the cost—He knew the hearts of those Pharisees and every detail of their plottings, yet He reached out to that guy anyway. Jesus could have waited till the Pharisees went to lunch or asked the guy to come back the next day; instead, He reacted in heroism, truth, and contempt for evil. He reacted in selflessness and an unearthly passion driven by an unearthly compassion. He reacted in all the character and magnificence of the man He truly was—God incarnate.

He saw the pain, He saw the need, He felt the heartache—and He touched that guy. And Jesus didn't heal in some macho display of self-righteousness—that's not what He was about. He loved the Pharisees, too, and He was constantly trying to get across to them as well that *people* were His Father's priority, and care for them was more important than what day it was; that the Father Himself was priority, and the Sabbath was supposed to be about Him and not the

145

other way around. It was Jesus' heartcry for those guys to understand Him as well, and trade in all their circumcisions of the skin for one, big, godly circumcision of the heart.

Imagine Jesus that day in the synagogue: He's excited to share a few truths with the packed house when in walk these teachers of the Law, dragging this poor guy along. They shove him in front, hoist his sleeve, and grandstand his deformity—"Is it lawful to heal on the Sabbath?" Think of the fear and shame Jesus saw reflected in this guy's eyes—I bet His heart was sliced raw. I can see a tear roll down His one cheek as He begs those Pharisees to loose the hardness from their hearts: "How much more valuable is a man than a sheep!" And I can see another tear roll down the other cheek as He turns to this fellow, takes that bent hand in His, and whispers, "Stretch out your hand."

I can picture this fellow seeing something in Jesus' eyes that makes him forget the whole room is staring—something that gives him the confidence to try it. He pushes, first the little finger, then the index— it moves! The arm is flexing! Fingers are growing. The pain—it's gone! What was dead flesh now lives!

He collapses, sobbing, into the arms of Jesus—this Man who smiled at him and reached out and actually touched his deformity. This Man who risked everything for ugly little him. This Man who told every-one in the room—the teachers of the Law and everyone—*he* was more important than even the *Sabbath*. This Man named *Jesus*!

You know, there were people who went home that day believing Jesus was Messiah, and there were others who went home not believ-ing. Regardless of how anyone felt, I can't imagine even one walked away unstunned—and that's not just because they witnessed a dis-play of miracle power that could only be of God, but also because they witnessed a display of love, humility, and heroism that could only be of God. Whatever anyone may have felt about Jesus that day, I have to believe there wasn't one who wasn't thinking, *Whoever this Guy is, wow, what a Guy!*

You know, we assume the miracle power of Jesus was the testimony of His Messiahship and the reason anyone chose to follow Him. I don't doubt that's largely true. But think about the "who He was" people saw out there when they hung in the shadows and watched His moves. Think about what must have gone through their minds when they saw Him turn to some wretched outcast everyone else despised when there were wealthy, beautiful, "righteous" folks standing there as well who anyone else would want to get close to. Surely it amazed them to see a Man who would make that extraordinary kind of choice, but that's the kind of man those first-century folks saw Jesus be every day of His life.

And did you ever notice how Jesus never used His power to destroy opposition or lavish Himself with luxuries? He could turn five fish sandwiches into 5000 and raise people from the dead; but never did He zap Himself a nice lobster dinner, or a cushy carriage, or anything like that—things most of us would do right away, given the chance. Where did Jesus exercise His power to do anything for himself? Nowhere! It must have blown the people's minds to see it: He *always* used His miracle power *only for other people*. What kind of remarkable man would make such a remarkable choice? Jesus, that's who.

And therein lies the difference between His priorities, motivations, idea of success, and ours. Yes, one huge discovery I made was how blindingly different a Man He was from us. But we could examine any day or encounter of Jesus' life and see the same things over and over: acts of giving, humility, care, integrity, sacrifice. Acts of superhuman selflessness, the tiniest of which, aside from causing the blind to see and the lame to walk, screamed to all who looked on, *This is God!* For there's no way such wholeness of character, such totality of love could possibly be that of a mere man.

Another favorite story about Jesus is one that wasn't recorded by Matthew, so I didn't get the chance to act it. But I love it, so I'll cheat a bit and tell it anyway. It's the story of the adulteress dragged before Jesus, when He spoke those startling words: "If any one of you is without sin, let him be the first to throw a stone at her." This story also tends to take on a sentimental quality in our imaginations and artistic representations, but one glance at the hard realities of the whole event and lukewarm quickly turns to sizzle and burn.

I'm struck with the "heat" surrounding Jesus the day it happened. The chapter before opens with Jesus staying away from Judea because the Jews were waiting to *kill* Him. No one would talk publicly about him for *fear* of the Jews. In the middle of His teaching, the crowd *accuses* Him of being *demon-possessed*, the talk swirling, "Isn't this the man they're trying to *kill?*" At one point temple guards are sent to *arrest* Him, and the Pharisees *fight* with Nicodemus about Him, and so on. I'm telling you, "hot" isn't a hot-enough word for the atmosphere whipping about Jesus that morning. The air must have been electric with tension.

But in spite of all that, there He sits in the temple courts, teaching at the crack of dawn. Unbelievable! The bravery, the zeal, the heroism of that alone is mind-boggling. Along come the big, bad Pharisees, using yet another human being as a pawn in their struggle for power— this time, shamefully so, *a woman.*

Can you imagine the terror of being manhandled the way she undoubtedly was—your intimacies shouted to the world, murder screamed in your face? Can you imagine the sheer violence of being ripped from your bed by a mob—screaming, clawing, kicking, fighting for your life? Can you imagine what she probably looked like by the time she was thrown at Jesus—shaking, bleeding, battered, delirious? What a gut-wrenching violation.

And how the crowd would have gotten into it. We all know how people rush to the scene of a fight or accident.

Now, I don't know what Jesus may have written in the dirt that day. I've heard lots of speculation, though none has ever seemed satisfactory. My personal opinion is He scribbled that woman a quick message, "Don't sweat it, kid. I'll have you out of this in no time."

Forgive me for that, but as I think about the pain that must have ripped through Jesus' heart seeing the inhumanity being heaped on this woman, and knowing the Pharisees' motives—His temperature must have blasted through the roof that morning. A rich mixture of temple wrath and shriveled-hand heartbreak must have boiled inside Him and exploded in a volcano of passion as He rose to face that mob—"If any one of you is without sin, let him be the first to throw a stone at her!" Subtext—*"Go ahead, make My day!"*

This was no serene "porcelain doll" Jesus, as Regardt puts it, who stood up to those guys that morning in the temple courts. He desperately loved that woman and hated the evil being perpetrated on her. And in a crowd full of people too scared to get involved, He rose, the only one courageous enough to say what needed to be said and do what needed to be done; the only one with enough integrity to stand for right and goodness in the face of the entire religious authority. Again He risked Himself—and all for the sake of one "nobody" sinner-of-a-woman whom obviously no one else cared about.

I often think about the guy she was in bed with—where was he when she needed him that morning? Why wasn't he defending her like Jesus was? No, he was there when he could get something out of it, but when asked to climb out of her bed and into her life, he was out the back door and down the street. Then there's Jesus—a *real* man—standing heroically between that woman and the mob that wanted to kill her, with nothing to gain and everything to lose—shielding her, protecting her, loving her—*being a Man to her.*

And after that crowd cooled and slinked away, I can see Jesus turning to that girl, covering her nakedness with whatever cloak He had, holding her as she shakes and sobs in relief. I have no doubt He wiped away her every tear and smiled into her eyes, "Then neither do I condemn you."

Oh, the compassion, the heart, the care, the courage—the Man, the God—*Jesus.*

Then there was the day He hung, beaten and dying, on a wooden cross. None of us can begin to imagine the pain, the trauma—His face a bloodied mess, His joints popping, His muscles tearing, His lungs wheezing and straining for each swallow of life-sustaining air.

He forces open swollen eyes and sees His mother crying in the arms of His friend, John. What a remarkable woman—she's stood by Him through it all. She's remained faithful through the cursing, the mocking, the laughing, the lying. She's stuck by Him through all the loneliness and rejection and betrayal and beating. She's feasted on His every victory, and now she's being force-fed His ultimate agony.

This woman means so much to Him. If there ever was one who encouraged Him, supported Him, believed in Him, and picked Him up when He was down—if there was ever one who understood and truly loved Him—it was this woman. She was there from the beginning, she was there through it all, and now she's here—at the "end."

He'd like to smile and let her know it's going to be okay, but His face is broken—He can't even feel it. In fact, He doesn't even know how much of it is still there. But He does know one thing—there's precious little time left, and there's something He needs to do. It's something so important He musters every ounce of strength He has to do it. He forces open His mouth, struggles against the bruised and torn tissues, looks to this woman and His buddy, and as the Gospel of John records, squeezes out as best He can, "Dear woman, here is your son . . ." and to John, "Here is your mother."

I had read those words countless times, but it wasn't until I took this journey through His life that I understood for the first time what they really meant—what He was *really* saying to His mother and this man from the cross that day.

There, in the middle of all the horror, in the middle of all the swelling and gasping and dying, He musters up enough strength to look down and essentially say:

Take care of My mama.

If there ever was a stunning display of the kind of man Jesus was 2000 years ago, that was it—in His final moments, through the blood in His teeth, "Take care of My mama." Like I said, *What a Guy.*

———————

His name was Jesus. On the surface, just a regular guy, but under the surface, not regular in the least—in fact, quite beyond remarkable.

And that's not just because He could raise a dead man with a sentence, or feed thousands with a handful of scraps, or even open eyes that had been sealed from birth. But also because He was a Guy you could count on—a solid Guy—a Guy you could trust. A humble, gentle Guy who would stop everything He was doing to care for you, no matter how dirty or messed up you happened to be. A heroic Guy who would stand up for you no matter how many stood against you. A giving, selfless Guy who would risk everything for you no matter the personal cost. An honest Guy who told it like it was and got killed for it. Simply put, the greatest Guy you'd ever want to meet—this guy named Jesus.

You know, when the whole adventure was done, I remember sitting with my journal, searching for some profound way to sum up how I felt about the whole experience. I sat for a long time, and finally, the only thing I could come up with was this:

I will miss You.

What can I say about that? He was the greatest Guy I'd ever met, and I'd fallen in love with Him, with who He was and how He lived His life, and with the special way I'd experienced it all. As crazy as I knew it sounded, as much as I knew He wasn't going anywhere, all I could think to say was I was going to miss Him. And as I sit here today, He's still the greatest guy I've ever met; and as crazy as it still sounds, I still really miss Him—that Guy named Jesus.

THE WAVE AND THE VOLCANO

CHAPTER TEN

"Lord, make me a puppet on your strings."

IT SEEMS ALMOST EVERY TIME I get interviewed I'm asked, "Why another Jesus movie? What makes *Matthew* different?" The answer to that question, first and foremost, has to be that *Matthew* is the Word of God—the Gospel in its entirety, undiluted by addition or deletion. That reality is undoubtedly its essence, its excitement, and its power.

But right alongside that, I've come to discover our creative approach was absolutely unique, even as far as making Jesus films goes: Regardt on his face seeking God for every decision and Bruce Rudnick, interceding and bringing the Word to Reg and me on a scene-by-scene basis. These were undoubtedly the nuts and bolts of the entire exercise.

Speaking of which, let me share a quick Bruce Rudnick story. It's one I generally keep to myself due to its potential for misunderstanding, but it's such an example of the myriad of ways God used Bruce out there, I'm going to take the risk. The story falls under the heading of "In case you thought I was some sort of spiritual giant, think again." Here goes nothing. . . .

153

It was late in the shoot and we were filming in the middle of South Africa's steaming summer heat. The producers had hired a few extra crew members for the home stretch, one of whom was a very attractive young lady. Well, you guessed it (boy, this is embarrassing!)—I found myself getting a little distracted every time she walked by.

The two of us never really talked outside of the standard "Hi, how's it going?" that usually takes place as two people cross paths during the course of a working day. Nothing was ever said or done; it's just that I found myself, like I said, a little distracted.

The problem, however, was this—I was getting more distracted with each passing day, and though it was not yet a big deal, it had the potential to become a very big deal. I was tired and alone and on the other side of the world . . . and you get the idea.

Early one morning I was sitting by our "Sea of Galilee" with my script and my coffee when Bruce walked up to me. He was sporting his standard smile and robust laugh as he bellowed, "Good morning, my bru! The Lord gave me a word for you this morning." He opened his Bible to the book of Proverbs and shared with me, "The one who winks at you plots your destruction."

"Does that mean anything to you?" Bruce asked.

"Not a thing," I replied.

"Well, the Lord will reveal it to you, because I'm certain it was from Him. Talk with you later!" He sauntered off to bury his hunger at the breakfast table, and I returned to my coffee by the lake.

It wasn't a minute later that our new crew member drove up. She looked her usual wonderful self and smiled broadly at me, no doubt matching the smile that was beaming back at her. Then, as she passed and said good morning, she did something she'd never done before that moment. You guessed it—*she winked at me!*

I couldn't believe my eyes! And as if that wasn't enough, *every* time she walked by that day she winked, again and again! She never once winked before that day or after, but that particular day she winked at me every single time we crossed paths. Unbelievable!

Talk about the fear of God getting into a person! It gave me the scare of my life, and all attraction for that woman immediately transformed into stark terror. From that morning on, I ran the other way as fast as my sandals could take me. I'm not saying that woman was knowingly plotting my destruction, but I sure think the Lord was protecting both of us. And that's just one tiny example of how Bruce was used by Him again and again to keep things on track.

With regard to Regardt's obedience to the Holy Spirit, many times he would walk onto the set with a scene meticulously mapped, then toss it all away in favor of what was developing spontaneously. The arrest scene is a good example. Reg came to me with a specific sequence, but by the time we were through rehearsal and the camera rolled, it had completely changed. There were countless times in the Sermon on the Mount scene alone when something would just kind of "happen" spontaneously, yet Regardt would go with it, sensing it was right. Not surprisingly, across the board those unplanned moments are among the most embraced in the film.

For example, there's the much-talked about "plank in the eye" scene, where Jesus grabs a huge staff and holds it to His face while teaching, "Why do you look at the speck of sawdust in your brother's eye, but pay no attention to the plank in your own eye?" It was a thing that "just happened" completely unplanned or even discussed. The camera was rolling, I was approaching that section of the speech, and the thought flashed through my mind, *There's a staff against that rock— use it for a plank in your eye!* My first reaction was, *It's on the other side of the mountain, and the cameraman's not expecting it!* But my second reaction was, *Go for it!* I ran across the mountain, the cameraman somehow kept focus, Regardt went with it, and the shot has become a revelation to folks—Jesus' mastery at teaching, hand-in-hand with His divine sense of humor.

And then there's the scene where I drenched Peter with water— Herrit still hasn't forgiven me for that. But in my defense, again, it was a thing that just happened. I was taking him the water bag to drink from, but there was so serious an expression on his face, and he was so obviously roasting in the sun—I just couldn't resist the impulse to wake him up and cool him down a bit (yeah, right!). Purely coincidentally, the line I was speaking at that moment was, "But when you give to the needy, do not let your left hand know what your right hand is doing." How funny can it get! Again, Reg went with it, and again it's proven to be one of those universally enjoyed moments, displaying Jesus as the down-to-earth, fun-loving Man He undoubtedly was.

The stories go on and on, but suffice it to say, alongside Regardt's devotion to the Word, the big difference in *Matthew* was his willingness to sacrifice control. Reg walked in constant anticipation and excitement about the Holy Spirit's grasping the reins and leading the proceedings, and that was his chosen method of directing every scene of every day.

As for me, I've mentioned how my constant prayer on the set was, "Lord, make me a puppet on Your strings." I used to plead with Him, "Show me what really happened that day, and take over my mouth, my body, my heart, and actually 'do' what You did that day."

Those are dangerous prayers, I know. But you must understand, I was totally ignorant of the hugeness of the things I was asking and so wholly aware of my own inadequacy.

I've told you the "Woe to Korazin" story. Surprise—that isn't the only scene where something like that happened. Many times during the filming a deluge of emotion/passion would rise in my gut and just explode—a complete surprise to me and everyone around me. I remember almost every time I talked in character about people going to eternal punishment, I would spontaneously lose it. Grief would rise in me like a sickness in my gut, and I'd come emotionally unglued. It happened time after time.

I remember sitting on the "temple" steps and telling the parable of the wedding banquet, where the king says to his servants, "Throw [that man] outside, into the darkness, where there will be weeping and gnashing of teeth." Out of nowhere, pain flooded into my heart, and I found myself struggling to grip my emotions. My voice cracked in belting, "For many are invited, but few are chosen!" It just killed me inside as I looked at the faces surrounding me. It was like this urgent heartcry—"Don't you see? You're marching into hell! Don't do it!" How desperately the Lord was trying to save them.

There was also the parable of the sheep and goats. When I got to the part, "Then he will say to those on his left, 'Depart from me, you who are cursed, into the eternal fire prepared for the devil and his angels,'" again a depth of grief enveloped my heart that I can't describe, and I could barely continue with the remainder of the speech. It was like a knife of pain thrust into my heart, and I fought with everything I had to get the final words out.

We did two takes on that speech, and on the first I just sat with my back against a wall and cried like a baby. When Regardt finally whispered, "Cut," everybody froze—nobody even breathed—and tears were rolling down the cheeks of many crew faces. The cameraman straightened up, his eyes sopping wet, and silently nodded at me over the eyepiece. Everyone was blown away at what had happened—including me.

Heartbreakingly, moments such as that one were sometimes lost to a technical error, or maybe a dropped word, or any number of pitfalls that are all a natural part of moviemaking. Nevertheless, they happened over and over again. Sometimes, too, one of those moments would end up on the proverbial cutting-room floor because "it just didn't cut right" into the final edit. A good example is a scene we shot for the "40 days in the wilderness" sequence. It was a close-up of me falling face-first into the dirt and coming up muddy and sweaty and pained and strained. For some reason, I just exploded in emotion and tears began to stream down my face. I struggled and fell again, groaning in anguish, trying to push myself up, spitting sand and gravel.

I'll never forget the crew's pain in watching it unfold—especially the makeup assistant, dear Khadija. She was literally weeping and came running to help me off the ground when the camera stopped rolling. Everyone knew we'd gotten a special piece of film, but when I sat down to watch the final edit, it was nowhere to be found. Reg told me it pained him to cut it, but in piecing the entire sequence together, the close-up didn't fit anywhere, and he was forced to leave it out.

But praise God—some of those scenes were captured and retained for all the world to see—two in particular, and they're what this chapter is about. If you're familiar with *Matthew* you probably know exactly which two they are: the "Woes" of Matthew 23, and the Garden of Gethsemane, or, as I've come to remember the experience of them, "The Wave and the Volcano."

We filmed both scenes during the final week of shooting, and as you can imagine, by that time I was beyond exhausted. Emotionally, physically, intellectually, spiritually—you name it, I was wrung out and running on empty.

This is the journal entry I wrote only midway through the shoot, upon arrival in Cape Town from Morocco: "I arrived in a state of

157

serious exhaustion, sleeping 21 of the first 24 hours here. Dehydrated, emotionally spent, and physically depleted. . . ."

Can you believe that? It's true—I arrived in my South African hotel room in the middle of a gorgeous summer afternoon, went straight from shower to bed, and awoke *21 hours* later! And I still had the second half of the shoot to go. I'd been living a six-days-a-week, 15-hours-a-day roller-coaster ride on the other side of the world, and I was feeling every second of it.

In fact, that's the best way to describe the whole adventure: It was like being on a wildly racing roller coaster for weeks on end, never stopping or even coming up for air. My heart was being yanked, broken, torn down, and reconstructed, over and over, day after day. There were nights when it ached so badly I'd just buckle on the floor of my hotel room and cry my eyes out.

Well, scheduled into that final week of shooting were some of my biggest scenes, the most grueling of which was undoubtedly Matthew 23—the seven "Woes." It was massive—an entire chapter—and it was very intimidating. From the moment I saw it on the schedule I began praying like a madman. Since Regardt intended to shoot it in its entirety from beginning to end, I gave every spare moment to reviewing the words for memory.

Reg brought in hundreds of extras, and a colorful Jerusalem crowd dressed the temple steps. The Pharisees and the Twelve were also out in force, and the crew was buzzing with the excitement that comes with shooting big scenes.

Two cameras would cover the action—one at the top of the steps and one on a crane at the bottom. The African sun was merciless that day, pounding on us and mirroring off the granite set as we all settled in for a walk-through technical rehearsal. "Jesus" was to step out from the crowd and onto the top step as the Pharisees stormed off, infuriated by His teaching. There He would belt His first "Woe to you!" and follow them all the way down the steps for the remainder of the speech—end of scene. It seemed a simple setup. But in the final analysis, it would prove to be anything but.

In that technical rehearsal I stepped onto the first step and began reciting the speech, casually walking through the action for camera with a cup of cold water dangling from my right hand. But a couple paragraphs into it, to my dismay, I drew a blank—I couldn't remember the words. Antoinette, the script supervisor, prompted me, but I drew another blank. She prompted me again, but I lost it again, and again, and again. . . .

Keep in mind, I had those words 100-percent memorized before I left L.A., and I'd reviewed them extensively in the days leading up to that rehearsal. But there I was, struggling to put two paragraphs together, and it seemed the harder I tried the worse it got. Exhaustion was winning the battle, and I couldn't do anything about it.

As you can imagine, I wasn't exactly thrilled about it. Regardt, on the other hand, was typically understanding. We had a quiet chat and he said, "Don't worry. We'll roll the cameras until you run out of words, then pick it up from there."

It sounded good, but it didn't make me feel much better. I felt as if I'd let Reg and the crew down, not to mention the Lord. And on top of that, it was plain embarrassing to drop the ball like that in front of all those people. But what could I do? The scene would have to get on film, even if that meant one word at a time; so I swallowed my pride in one huge lump and prepared to grind my way through it as soon as Reg was ready.

Blessed Cape Tonians—many had come to be crowd-extras for no pay just to be a part of what God was doing. I can see their faces as if it were yesterday—all sizes and shapes, all colors and cultures, men and women, kids and grannies. They were all out there that day, and I know they were praying for me as they watched me struggle.

I came to discover the "other camp" was there as well. I didn't know it during the shoot, but there were actually satanists on some locations praying destruction over us—this day in particular.

After we'd finished filming, a crew member told me he was relaxing back at the equipment trucks when he decided to wander over to the set and check out the action. There was a pillar behind which he could strategically watch without getting in the camera line, so he leisurely parked himself there and settled in. Oddly, he noticed a book lying open on the ground at the base of this pillar, but other than thinking it strange, he gave it no particular attention.

Then something happened—he wasn't standing there for ten seconds when he felt what he described as a "huge, freezing, icy claw" grip his spine. He said it was as sickening a feeling as he'd ever experienced (you should have seen his face when he tried to explain it to me). Not knowing what it was or where it came from, he just turned and ran back to the trucks. As he did so, it left him.

He returned to the set for another look an hour later. His best vantage point was that same pillar, so not thinking anything about it, he went back to the same spot—mistake.

The first thing he noticed was that book still lying open. Again he thought it odd but paid it no mind. Then it happened a second time— that same icy claw gripping his spine and shooting waves of sickening frozenness throughout his body. This time, though, he told me it was twice as intense and twice as awful.

He turned to bolt out of there again, but as he did so, he looked down at that book, and what he saw shook his soul. It was a book by a guy named Aleister Crowley—satanist; self-proclaimed "the most evil man on earth." The crewman told me that when he saw that, stark fear came over him and he silently mouthed, *They're here*. Then the dynamics of the whole thing hit him—"Jesus" on the "temple" steps, and this, right there as well. He ran trembling back to the trucks and never went near that pillar again.

Now if you find that a little hard to believe, let me tell you—this guy was a nonbeliever. He was a nice, easygoing, completely-void-of-agenda kind of guy. He told me he'd never before mentioned the story to anyone because he was too afraid to talk about it. You should have seen his eyes—they were as big as doughnuts.

But praise God—the Lord protected us from beginning to end. Glory to His precious Name!

Getting back to the seven "Woes"—there I was with the cameras about to roll, unable to put two paragraphs together. And there was another problem facing me, as well—that same "Woe to Korazin" dilemma.

Jesus is again saying some very heavy stuff—probably the harshest things we have record of Him saying, calling these Pharisees everything from snakes to dead men's bones. It kind of makes "Woe to Korazin" look like a tea party. How could I accurately speak, as the ever-compassionate Jesus, words that appeared so downright vicious and hate-filled? How does a guy lovingly call someone a snake? It was well beyond me, so again I did the only thing I could think to do: pray.

Boy, did I pray. I stood on the edge of that set, my back to the hundreds that were milling about, sweat dripping off my nose, gazing over the expanse of Cape Town below, begging the Lord to rescue the situation one more time. "I don't know what to do, Lord! I can't even remember the words! I need You to take over! Oh, dear God, *make me a puppet on Your strings!*"

I have no idea how long I prayed—it felt like forever—and if I wasn't exhausted going into that prayer, I was knocked out coming out of it. Eventually, though, Diana, the first assistant director, gingerly approached, "We're ready to try one, Bruce." I took a final swallow of water and ascended the granite steps to my first position.

We would back into the previous speech and overlap into the Woes. A blanket of silence dropped over the set, I mumbled one last desperate plea heavenward, and Regardt called, "Action!"

"Whoever exalts himself will be humbled, and whoever humbles himself will be exalted." The Pharisees turned away and I followed, cutting through the multitudes and emerging at the top of the steps, "Woe to you, teachers of the law and Pharisees, you hypocrites!"

Somewhere shortly beyond those opening lines, something happened that I'm at a loss to adequately explain. I remember the Pharisees turning their backs on me, and the only way I can describe what happened next is to say it was like getting hit from behind by a huge wave.

You know how you're swimming at the ocean and that happens? You get hit by a wave you weren't expecting or weren't ready for, and suddenly you're caught helplessly in the whitewater, tumbling and not knowing which end is up, reaching for the surface, clawing for air. Then finally you're washed onto the shore and you can breathe, and you look around and realize where you are, and everything is finally okay.

That's the only way I can think to describe the experience, and it was to such an extent I hadn't the slightest idea of anything I was doing or saying or even where I was. All I know is that suddenly I was on my knees, alone, and crying my eyes out. I remember feeling so emotionally naked in front of all those people—I could barely move, and it was all so awful.

I looked up and there was Kevin, "John the Beloved," standing a distance away, frozen and staring with the most strained expression. I remember feeling so broken and needing someone desperately, so I lifted a hand to him as if to say, *Help me.* It was a completely unscripted moment. He didn't move for the longest time, then finally came and held me and took me away. Neither of us realized it, but the cameras were still rolling, capturing the entire exchange.

Kevin took me off the set and I just cried, heartbroken beyond heart break, and not even knowing why. Regardt came and told me I'd done the *entire scene*—this scene whose words I couldn't remember and couldn't figure how to act. It was all over—the "Woes" were in the can.

My journal entry reads:

March 26.

The Holy Spirit swept me up in the woes, and I broke big-time. It was exciting, as the words came straight from the Lord, and the emotions flowed as I wept for Israel—all captured on film. Extras and onlookers wept. The Lord has really moved in many scenes in a strong and deliberate manner—the world through His eyes. The cost is high in emotions, but the intimacy with Jesus is worth every heartache.

What happened that day on the set is so humbling, so remarkably tender. Watching it for the first time in an editing room with Regardt, I couldn't believe my eyes. I'd broken in so deep a place, it pained me to sit through it.

The Lord wasn't spitting fire at these guys—He was *loving* them. His rage was not a self-righteous "Now you've had it!" It was the rage one experiences watching someone he loves walk out the door. It was a rage *born of a broken heart*. It was His last-ditch effort to gain them—desperately holding a mirror to their faces, passionately heartcrying for them, having done everything He could to make them see and understand, "*I am He! And I love you! Don't do what you're doing! Come to Me!*"

O Jerusalem, Jerusalem . . .
how often I have *longed* to gather your children together,
as a hen gathers her chicks under her wings,
but you were not willing.
Look, your house is left to you desolate.

How Jesus treasured and desired them; how He wept over their self-destruction. The broken heart of Jesus—so much deeper than any of us can imagine.

A gentleman was at the filming who managed the facility we used for these temple scenes. He was so excited to have us there, he didn't miss one moment of the action, snapping happily with his camera, always coming around to chitchat. I remember him as a jolly man, always smiling. But that day, when I fell on my knees and wept those words, "O Jerusalem, Jerusalem . . ." I was told that he broke down sobbing and ran away. Little did any of us know, he was belovedly Jewish. I never saw him again after that.

The scene had another influence I didn't know about until ten months later, when I was speaking in a little seaside Cape Town church hall. I opened the floor for questions, and immediately a very hard-looking man stood and belted, "I don't have a question; I have something to say." *Uh-oh*, I thought. He stepped into the aisle and began walking toward me. *Lord, get me out of this one!*

The closer the guy came, the more familiar he looked, though I couldn't quite place him. Then he said it—"I played a Pharisee in *Matthew*," and it hit me—this guy was the one Pharisee on the set who got under my skin. He was gruff and foul-mouthed, and he irritated the tunic off of me. I mean, here I was trying to concentrate on playing Jesus, and here was this guy at the coffee table, swearing. Though told to stop time after time, his cursing was a habit, I guess, because it wasn't long before he was singing out again. It got so irritating I came within inches one day of asking Regardt to fire the guy.

Well, here he was walking toward me, and when I realized who he was, my prayers went up twice as fast: *O, Lord! I need You now!* Then he was speaking to the entire congregation, "Not long ago, I wouldn't be caught dead in a place like this. I hated God and I hated anything that had to do with Him. If I were in a church meeting, I'd be heckling and making fun and laughing at all you fools and trying to mess the meeting up."

He pulled up next to me and looked me in the eye. "But one day on the set, you were standing on the temple steps, shouting, 'Woe to you!' and I looked up, and I don't know how to explain it, but suddenly it wasn't you anymore—*it was God*—and God was talking right at me. I went home that day and gave my life to Jesus Christ."

What can I say? I'm going to spend eternity with that "Pharisee." And if his one soul was what the whole *Matthew* experience was about, then it was worth every tear, every drop of sweat, and then some. Amen and Amen. Later in the evening, he privately told me how his wife had died shortly after the filming. "She was my whole life," he confided. "If I didn't have Jesus, I would have killed myself right then and there." The Lord knew that. And again, Amen.

———————

We shot another scene that final week; in fact, it was the very last scene in the entire shoot—the Garden of Gethsemane.

To say I was overwhelmed by this scene would be the understatement of the decade. I'd done my research and quickly concluded there was no way I or any other actor could even begin to approach the depth of Jesus' agony in the garden. Not even Pacino, De Niro, and Marchiano combined (who's Marchiano?) could pull off a thing like that. To say the least, I was in way over my head on this one.

All the Garden scenes were originally scheduled for the second-to-last week of shooting, in an olive grove nestled in the magnificent Paarl winelands of the Cape. We would start at sundown and work through the night until everything was in the can, finishing with scenes 249/251: Gethsemane Prayer Spot/Resume Gethsemane Prayer Spot.

From the moment I saw them on the schedule, I began to go through a Gethsemane of my own, agonizing over the impossibility of it all. I went around to everyone and privately begged, "Pray for me, man— I'm nowhere on this one." And as we worked through the schedule that night, I'd slip into the grove at every opportunity for some praying of my own.

The arrest scene, however, really got my mind off of the agony of Gethsemane. It was a big, important, exciting scene and I was having the time of my life walking through it. The physical logistics were difficult to coordinate, and we painstakingly worked rehearsal after rehearsal, trying to find what was working and what wasn't. The clock was ticking fast, but eventually Regardt was certain everything was right, and the cameras rolled.

You know, it was so breathtaking to be reenacting these most significant events in human history, and for some reason that really hit me during the arrest scene. I was completely overwhelmed with the absolute wonder of it all. Here was "Judas" walking toward me, kissing me on the cheek and speaking words that shook the very core of creation, "Greetings, Rabbi." In a heartbeat I would throw a grip over his shoulder and whisper, "Friend, do what you came for." Those are as huge as moments get—redemption itself was hanging in the balance. Between takes, I turned to "Mary Magdalene" (actress Pippa Duffy) and said, "Can you believe what we're doing?" She responded, "I know—it's unbelievable!" To this day I can still see the wonder on her face as she said that.

But as the shots were put in the can that night, we drew closer to the inevitable Gethsemane prayer scenes. My research notes read, "Point of climax of inner conflict. Physically unable to hold Himself up—so agonized. 'My Father/Abba'—a cry of 'Daddy!' from a child (the most intimate way to refer to your dad for the Jews)." There was no way I could even come close to Jesus' depth of agony, His heartcry that night, and I knew it. Not only that, I was so exhausted that my emotions were completely dried up. I remember sitting with Bruce

Rudnick on a slab of granite under a wild olive tree as they were set-ting lights, and saying, "I don't have it in me to do this scene, brother." All he could suggest was to pray.

Finally it was time. Diana sensitively cleared all nonessential per-sonnel from the set, and Regardt walked me through the action as the remaining crew hushed. I told Reg it wasn't happening for me, and his tender words in reply were, "We've got all night to do it. Whenever you're ready, just let me know." I dropped back in a cover of trees and again begged the Lord for a miracle.

Colin Polson, our makeup artist, approached me. Colin had become a special friend, not to mention the finest makeup artist I had ever worked with. Over the hours and days and weeks, Colin had gotten to know me very well. He knew exactly how to read and handle me, and when I was feeling tense or pressured, he would see it in my eyes, ask Diana for time, and pretend to touch me up just to give me a breather. I'll never forget his pretending to fuss with my hair, whisper-ing in my ear, "You're doing great. Slow down. Don't try so hard. . . ." Colin wasn't just a great makeup artist, but one of the best acting coaches I've ever had as well.

But as I stood pacing and praying that night, Colin approached me with a tiny squeeze bottle I'd never seen and said something he'd never said before. He held up that little bottle and asked, "Do you want some tears?"

Artificial tears! Call it pride if you must, but to me, as an actor, that's an embarrassment to even consider. But the look in Colin's eyes and the mere fact he suggested it confirmed what I already knew: I was dry as a bone, and I needed help. I'm ashamed to admit it, but resigning myself to the indignity, I gave Colin the go-ahead. Without a word, he squirted a touch in each eye, and the tears began to flow. Though I had no real emotion going, I tried to work up what I could and yelled, "Ready," to Regardt, knowing full well I wasn't anywhere close. He immediately responded with, "Action!" and I stumbled toward camera.

Then a miracle happened: It started to rain. It had been misting all night, but as the scene began, mist turned to drops and drops to heavy rain. I continued doing take after take without cutting, and surprisingly,

167

some nice emotion actually broke through. But then the sky opened wide and Regardt cut the scene as everyone ran for cover. The weather showed no sign of changing, so we packed the equipment and wrapped for the night.

The second assistant director approached me and said, "You're an amazing actor, Bruce. I've never seen anyone who could do what you just did." Regardt reassured me as well: "Some of it was forced, but there was definitely a lot we can use." Nodding an obligatory thanks to both, deep inside I knew that I'd fallen well short of the mark.

It was probably around 4:00 A.M., and the 45-minute drive back to the hotel was silent except for the clatter of rain dancing on the wind-shield. I remember sitting in the passenger seat, staring out at the blackness, trying to make myself feel better: *It's too late now, Bruce. Trust God with it. . . .* I came up with every feel-good cliché in the book, but my heart just ached for the opportunity to have a second go at it.

Well, I can't recall if I prayed for that second go specifically or not, but have a second go I did. After a few days, Regardt announced the rain had rendered the footage on scenes 249/251 unusable, and we'd have to reshoot them.

Hallelujah! I shouted on the inside, followed by an equally heartfelt *Uh-oh.* Yes, I would have another shot at it, but yes, I'd also have to face the same challenge all over again. Reg rescheduled the scenes as the final two of the shoot, just a short week away.

That final week reared its head much too quickly. I had dreaded it not so much because it meant facing those difficult scenes, but because it meant the adventure was coming to a close. It had been the most astounding, God-filled, purposeful, grand, and glorious experience of a lifetime and I didn't want to *ever* see it end, let alone in the next few days.

Still, feelings or no, the final night of shooting arrived. Contrasting my heavy heart, the crew enjoyed a general air of celebration. Yes, it had been marvelous for them as well, but it had also been a long, arduous haul, and most everyone was looking forward to getting back to normal life. I overheard one conversation where a crew member said exactly that: "I can't wait to get back to my life." In my own thoughts I responded, *This is my life.*

And so it was. Good or bad, healthy or not, *Matthew* had ceased to be a job or a ministry or anything I was "doing"—it had become my life. And whether I liked it or not, it would all come to an end before the sun rose on a new day.

Prior to tackling Gethsemane, though, the crew was busy shooting two of Peter's denials in the temple courtyard. Being the only one uninvolved, I grabbed a cup of coffee, pulled up a chair, and settled in for what would be a three-hour wait.

It was a gloriously warm summer night, and I'll never forget those hours, sitting in that plastic chair with my feet propped on a rock, gazing over Cape Town's city lights gently filtered through a forest of trees. It was absolutely magical.

The set was buzzing with visitors out to catch a final taste of what had meant so much to so many, but I stayed hidden on the edge of that forest, nestled tightly between two equipment trucks. It wasn't a time for conversation or picture taking; it was a time to be alone with my thoughts and my God—a time to drink in every last moment of this precious adventure He'd so blessed me with.

Now and again someone would pass, calling, "Has anyone seen Bruce?" I dared not move a muscle lest my hiding place be discovered and the intimacy spoiled. I was thanking my Lord and savoring the coarse texture of the robes that had become such a joy for me to be wrapped in—robes I'd be forced to relinquish in a very short while.

Then something wonderful happened. A huge buck emerged from the forest, not a stone's throw away. Being a wildlife fanatic, his powerful grace stole my breath away. I'd been sitting so still for so long he must have mistaken me for part of the scenery because he wandered closer and closer, actually coming within five or six feet of me. He never looked at me, just calmly grazed, completely unaware that he was putting on a show for one very alone American actor. I sat frozen, watching that big fellow for probably 30 minutes. It was such

169

a gift from God, like peeking into one of heaven's windows. Eventually he turned and grazed his way back into the bush, and the miracle was memory.

The Lord knew I was sitting there that night; He knew what was going on in my heart; He knew my love for His creatures—and He just blessed me. That magnificent animal's silent beauty brought such calm and absolute glory—it was as if the Lord Himself had paid me that visit, gently reassuring me. *Thanks for that, Lord; it meant so much to me that night.*

Finally, voices in the distance told me that the denial scenes were finished and the crew was preparing for Gethsemane. I wandered toward the location, but drawing near I could see the crowd of spectators had gotten huge, so I plopped behind a nearby tree, hiding in the cover of darkness until Regardt absolutely needed me.

One of the executive producers and his wife, Johan and Annelie Posthumus, coincidentally stumbled upon me with their faithful dog, Otto, in tow. We sat in the grass lightly chatting, but they easily sensed my fragility and graciously slipped off to join the others.

Finally I could hear Diana's voice crackling over a dozen walkie-talkies, "Bruce/Jesus—we're ready for Bruce/Jesus. . . ." That was my cue, so I stepped into the light and made myself known. It was a big moment in every way—I was standing at the exit door of the most remarkable time in my life, and Diana's face told me I wasn't the only one who felt that way. But there was no time for either of us to dwell on it. There was one last scene to put in the can, and it was a biggie; so we all turned our focus toward Gethsemane.

With the crew still setting a few last-minute lights, I began pacing a darkened dirt path just below them—an ideal spot to pray and prepare. In spite of the week's reprieve and the second chance, the scene still looked impossible. There wasn't one drop of moisture in either tear gland, nor one breath of strength in my heart.

And so I prayed. Oh, how I prayed. Pacing back and forth, I pleaded with the Lord to do a miracle—to one last time, "Make me a puppet on Your strings."

Diana cleared the set as best she could, but many of the spectators refused to be deprived of this final moment and remained. The crew took their positions, Diana yelled for everyone to settle, and quiet like you've never heard quiet fell over the hillside. Regardt approached—I can still hear the crunch of leaves splitting the silence beneath his every step as he walked from behind the camera and crossed the grass toward me.

There was a rock retaining wall along the hillside of the path. Regardt crouched on the top of it, I leaned my elbows on it, and the two of us shared what stands to this day as 20 of the most heartfelt minutes of my entire life. Not a soul moved as actor-director, brother-brother, two men who had grown from total strangers in a Los Angeles hotel lobby to the closest of friends, stood silently in the Cape summer breeze.

Regardt picked at the grass; I stared up the hill. Neither breathed a word for the longest time; then one of us, I don't remember who, simply said, "Well . . . this is it."

I can't remember much else of what was said. I remember we thanked each other and expressed our love for each other and our hope that it was all just a beginning rather than an end. It was one of those times when there really was nothing to say, simply because there was so much to say.

We talked about the scene—I told Him I was dry, and he said they'd wait for me all night, if need be. We prayed together, both about the scene and in thanksgiving for all that had taken place. Then time just sort of hung still, as neither of us wanted to let any of it go.

Finally a misty-eyed Diana, who still had a job to do, stepped in and nudged us with the sensitive whisper—"Standing by." It was a phrase she was renowned for, and I could tell by the tenor of her voice she was fully aware this would be the last time she said it.

Reg and I also had a job to do, so I jumped up to him and we walked through the action. It was simple—I would walk a line toward the camera about 20 feet, drop at the base of a tree, and play out the agonies. Regardt assured me again, "We'll wait for you—just shout when you're ready." I asked for Bruce Rudnick, and Diana rushed to call him. Reg and I shared a final "I love you, bro," and he slipped into the darkness behind camera.

Bruce came running—what a tremendous guy. I told him I couldn't find any emotion; he pointed to the city below and in vintage Bruce fashion said, "Just think about them and all the hurt that's going on down there right now. Do it for them." He placed a big hand on each of my shoulders and prayed, "Oh, Jesus, give my brother Your heart."

Colin approached with that squeeze bottle again, but this time I turned him down. Reg returned and said, "Let's try one and see what happens." Bruce gave me a hug, and both he and Reg disappeared behind the lights. Alone again, I offered a final desperate plea, "Lord God, just do it!" then called, "Ready, Reg!"

Diana immediately belted, "Quiet down!" Then, in a succession of all-too-familiar voices snapping from behind the lights—"Roll sound! Rolling! Mark it! *Action!*"

I walked into the shot, moving toward the tree Regardt had indicated. I was maybe five steps into it when something just exploded inside of me. The only way I can describe it is to say it was like a volcano of emotion erupting from inside, and all I can remember is the sensation of being literally *swallowed* in unimaginable grief—like helplessly collapsing and falling, being sucked into horror and consumed by it.

It was beyond awful, distress beyond distress, and I remember being completely unable to stop it. Just as in the "Woes," I had no awareness of anything I was doing or saying. All I can remember is pain—voluminous, engulfing *pain.*

Suddenly Regardt was there and he had his arms around me. Whatever had happened, whatever I'd done, it was over. Tears filled his eyes.

"What happened?" I asked.

"You did the scene."

"Both prayers?"

"Both prayers."

There would be no second take. Scenes 249 and 251 were in the can.

A week later, a group of investors gathered to see some footage. Reg invited me, and we all crowded into an editing room. Regardt chatted with us a while, then ran a few uncut scenes on the monitor—the arrest, a healing, a parable. As you can imagine, I had one eye on the screen and one on the investors. There was a whisper here and there, an occasional nod, a "Hmmm," a chuckle. Then the room got suddenly very still and uncomfortably hot—Regardt was running scenes 249 and 251—Gethsemane.

It was the first time I'd seen them—the first time anyone had seen them. Only then did I discover what had happened on that Cape Town hillside that night—the agony, the horror—and I had to turn my face away from the screen at the sight of it. Others did, too. It was so very awful.

173

But you know what I love most about what happened in the scene? Even more than the agony? The triumph that came with, "May your will be done"—a freshly focused Jesus, crippled in grief just moments before, rising like a mountain of a Man, a *champion*, brimming with courage, ready to march headlong into whatever lay before Him. In submission to the Father, He climbs from His brokenness with granite resolve to tackle the mission before Him, the ultimate expression of everything His life is all about—*the cross!*

After the film was released, *Matthew*'s scriptwriter came to me, zeroing in on that very thing. He exclaimed, "That bit of business after the last prayer—it was some of the greatest acting I've ever seen!" Well, that's flattering and I'd love to take the credit, but little did he know—little does anyone know—*I didn't have the slightest idea what I was doing at the time.* To quote Johan Posthumus, who watched that night, "I don't get it, Bruce. You had nothing—*I could see you had nothing.* Then suddenly . . . I don't get it."

It's called the Holy Spirit—about that, I have no doubt. And it's as humbling and inexplicable a thing as anyone could imagine. If the acting was brilliant, the credit doesn't go to me or anyone else—it goes to the *Holy Spirit.*

———————

As the crew packed the equipment that final night and everyone slapped congratulations on each other's backs, I slowly strolled from the set to the wardrobe truck. Sadness hung heavy in my heart as I silently untied my sandals and slipped out of my robes—for the last time.

With the crew's celebration going on behind me, I folded everything into a neat little stack and sat next to it on the back of the truck. I offered a simple prayer in that moment—*Thank You, Lord. Thank You for everything.* And with my hand placed firmly on those robes, I asked Him to someday give me the opportunity to wear them again.

I don't know exactly how long I sat there—it was quite awhile, that's for sure. But despite my heart, I couldn't sit there forever—eventually I would have to leave those robes behind. So finally, I swallowed hard, forced my gaze forward, rose to my feet, and stepped into the night.

My journal entry, recorded upon returning to my hotel room, simply reads:

March 31. *It is finished.*

And so it was.

THE CROSS

CHAPTER ELEVEN

For the joy set before him. . . .

HEBREWS 12:2

Journal: February 9

I hung on the cross yesterday. More when I have the time, but simply, I never began to understand what Jesus did for me until yesterday. And I still gained only a glimpse of the reality, the absolute subjection/submission to horror . . . for me. Every believer should wear a crown of thorns and hang on a cross for ten seconds—they would never be the same. And I can't help but feel that every non-believer would accept Christ on the spot if he did the same.

I have never felt so alone, so naked, so ugly, so emotionally bare—and I was just play-acting, dipping my toe into the experience of the cross. What He did for us! He chose it!

People were horrified by what they saw in my makeup and demeanor. I could see people all around me, disgusted.

Lying on that cross while people were huddling over me, being force-fed vinegar, seeing huge quantities of blood on my arm and on the ground. I looked at my arm and wept. Bruce read Scripture to me, and I wept. Waiting for lights to be hung, I wept. The Roman soldiers beat me, and I wept. Sitting alone in my loincloth, I wept. "Eloi, Eloi, lama sabachthani," and I wept. And as the stories come in from crew and onlookers, I'm discovering many wept. What He did for us. . . . Lives will never be the same. Mine will never be the same.

Hanging on the cross. It was awful beyond description—and I was faking it.

*I*F THERE'S A DAY in my history I can point to and say, "My life will never be the same," it is the day I hung from a wooden cross, high atop a barren hill overlooking Quarzazate. Other than stepping into salvation, it stands as my life's most turning-point experience.

Exactly how or why, I'm at a loss to explain. I doubt I'll ever truly understand the spiritual and soulful realities of what went on that day. So when it comes to describing the whole thing for you, all I can do is simply tell what little my memory affords and trust the Holy Spirit to work in your heart whatever it is He desires for you: "Lord, where my words fall so short of the mark, here, work sovereignly in spite of them. Amen."

Before we get into the actual stories, let me underscore the magnitude of the whole *Matthew* experience. Keep in mind this was no Hollywood Bible movie script—this was the gospel of Jesus Christ, "the power of God unto salvation," the living "does not return empty" Word of God, as recorded by Matthew under the hand of the Holy Spirit. It just doesn't get any bigger than that, and that's what we were in the center of out there—the Word of God studied, memorized, and on some tiny level actually "walked through" in reenactment.

Then to take that ultimate step—*the cross!* We're talking about the single moment every letter and comma in the Word turns on—everything that went before leads up to it, and everything afterward flows out of it. It's the single most tremendous release of power and glory in all of history, a moment that singlehandedly holds the universe from being ripped apart like a dirty old rag. It's a moment of such incomprehensible magnitude, it alone pays the penalty for every single wrong—every war and mass murder to every stolen pencil—in universal history from Day 1 on.

Given all that (and so much more), can you imagine the spiritual dynamics of what we knock-kneed filmmakers were involved in that cold February day? Never will I forget the pasta lunch Regardt, F.C., Bruce, and I had the following afternoon in a little cafe. We sat so all-amazed. "I wonder what it looked like above our heads yesterday?" "I'm not so sure I want to find out!" "Praise God for the victory, guys!" (That last comment, of course, coming from Regardt.)

Keeping those things in mind, let me take you now to the day we filmed Jesus before Pontius Pilate, a scene we shot several weeks after the crucifixion, using the Greco-Roman architecture of the University of Cape Town as the governor's domain.

Remember how I mentioned an actor's analysis involves looking at what his character does and asking the question, "Why?" As I contemplated this trial scene, that was my approach. I looked at what Jesus did before Pilate and asked, "Why did He do those specific things?" or more significantly, "Why did He *not do* the *things He could have?*"

Think about it. Jesus is the Son of the Living God. He'd performed countless miracles displaying power beyond anyone's comprehension—all the power of heaven and earth combined and beyond, in fact. Surely as He stood before Pilate that day, He had that same power waiting at His fingertips. If He wanted, He could have done some equally amazing things in front of everyone that day. He could have snapped His divine fingers and turned the whole bunch of them into a pack of baboons if He wanted. At the very least, He could have spoken up for Himself.

But as Matthew records it, with all those options available, Jesus stood silent that day, doing and saying nothing. That is, with one exception: When Pilate asks Him, "Are you the king of the Jews?" Jesus responds, saying, "Yes, it is as you say," or in other words, "Yes, I am Messiah." Other than that, *nothing.*

Now I had to sit back in my chair and take a hard look at that. *Why? He could have done anything that day, so why that one particular thing? After all* (and this is the big key), *if anybody has a choice, it's the Son of the Living God.*

It had never occurred to me before—Jesus actually having a choice about anything. But as an actor portraying Him, it became so stunning a revelation, so cornerstone fundamental—*this is the Son of God we're talking about, and if anyone in this world has a choice, it's Him!*

I'll never forget hanging on that cross, with this centurion looking up at me saying, "Come down from the cross, if you are the Son of God! (Ha-ha-ha!)" Looking down at that guy, it hit me like a ton of bricks—*He could have!* He could have given that guy one dirty look and turned him into an eggplant. He could have decided right then and there, "I've had enough of these people spitting in my face—they aren't worth it. And that Marchiano character who's going to treat me like dirt for most of his life. Forget it! I'm outta here!" But He didn't. He *chose* to just hang there.

So here's Jesus, standing before Pilate, saying that one thing, "Yes, it is as you say." It was the same line He'd spoken in front of the Jewish authorities the night before. *Why?*

I'm no theologian or authority, but as I looked at the practical dynamics confronting Jesus that day—at what was at stake—as I researched and went to my knees, it hit me:

> That one thing Jesus said that day—
> it was the one thing that was going to get Him *killed*.

That was the blasphemy; that was the offense; that was the reason they wanted to kill Him—He claimed to be the Son of God. And Jesus knows that. He knows as long as He continues to say that one thing, they're going to kill Him. Yet it is that one thing He intentionally chooses to say, "Yes, it is as you say."

Suddenly that image of a poor, helpless Jesus—a victim of these cruel, jealous men—disappeared in a heartbeat. Suddenly I saw a Jesus who was not a victim at all, but who was actually *controlling* the situation every step of the way, a Jesus who was intentionally pushing the specific buttons that would drive them to execute Him! He knew the fulfillment of His mission, and He knew what He had to do to get there. So there He is, acting helpless and defeated but actually pulling the strings on the entire event, playing everyone like puppets, straight into His plan for salvation.

Yes, Jesus was the one in charge that day—not Pilate nor the Pharisees nor anyone else for that matter—it was Jesus! Those guys thought they had Him, *but He had them*—reacting frame for frame just as He wanted so He'd be sure to end up exactly where He needed to be— *the cross.*

It's so vital a thing for us all to grasp: Jesus wasn't forced to the cross—He *chose* the cross.

And on that day, that most awful of days, He wasn't dragged to the cross. He was *crawling to* the cross. His battered body was giving out on Him; He had little life remaining in Him; yet He *had to make it* to the cross. Fighting against the pain, struggling, clawing, groping, crawling with everything He had—*one more step, one more step . . . almost there . . . one more . . . made it!*—and the hammer drops.

The cross. I don't know about anyone else, but before *Matthew* I hadn't the slightest idea of what truly happened that day. Perhaps, like other things we've discussed, it got watered down and prettied-up in too much familiarity, art, and sentimental pageantry. On top of that, there's a tendency to think along the lines, *Well, Jesus was God, and what could really hurt God? And besides, the angels were helping Him, and He knew He was going to be raised in a few days, so it probably wasn't a big deal for Him.*

But I must tell you, if I learned anything the day I hung on a cross for nine hours in Morocco, I learned it was a *very* big deal. I learned this day 2000 years ago just outside Jerusalem was nothing like those romantic paintings or airy reflections at all. I learned there was nothing pretty or poetic or our definition of "glorious" about it. I learned it was nothing less than awful—awful beyond your wildest imaginings.

The Bible says clearly that they beat Jesus so badly you couldn't even tell He was a human being. His face was "marred beyond human likeness" (Isaiah 52:14). Because one of Regardt's prime directives was to film "reality" as opposed to "religion," when it came to these scenes he sat with Colin and the guiding Scriptures and explained what he wanted me to look like.

Of course, as far as Colin would go—and he went further than anyone has gone—he couldn't come close to showing what it truthfully looked like. To do so would have gotten the film an X rating for excessive violence, and that was a line he had to be careful not to cross. So early one Quarzazate morning in a room at the hotel, he sat me down with his glue, paraffin, "blood," and dirt and went to work.

181

Usually a morning in Colin's chair was full of jokes and laughs, but this morning was different. There was nothing to joke about this morning. This was serious stuff, and it was to be handled that way. I knew it; Colin knew it; we all knew it.

Colin worked like a surgeon—quietly, soberly, certainly. I don't recall that he spoke outside the necessary, "Look up, please . . . This is going to feel tight . . . Close your eye, please . . ."

I have no idea how long I was in his chair that morning. I remember it was freezing cold as the sunrise-wind whipped through an open door behind him. Other than that, my mind was far away—2000 years away. While Colin brutalized my face with makeup, I prayed, silently begging the Lord to recreate Golgotha, to bring all the elements together, to anoint Regardt for his decisions, and, of course, to make me a puppet on His strings.

Readiness, terror, excitement, awe, reverence, inadequacy—it was all screaming through me. I remember feeling very much on edge, and the sobriety with which everyone worked created a mood in some odd way, as if what they were preparing me for was more real than anything else.

As Colin's glue and wax took over, my face gave way to twisting and distortion. I couldn't see it but I could feel it. My right eye was sealed shut, and my left eyelid was glued open. I could feel the caking of wax in and around my nose and ears, and the swelling plastered on my jaw. Colin brushed glue across my mouth, which cracked and peeled as it dried and tightened, making my lips feel torn and split.

With every glob of paraffin, with every clot of red stuff, with every drop of everything Colin was doing to me, I could feel my face getting more and more bent and maimed. By the time he was finished, it felt so literally beaten up that I had little actor's imaginative work to do.

I will never forget walking out of that makeup room and toward the car. First there was the desk clerk. He looked at me and literally fell against the wall, recoiling in horror. Then the doorman came running, grabbing me, yelling in a mix of Arabic and broken English, "What happened!" Colin assured him it wasn't real, but he just kept roaring and trying to somehow help me.

It was that awful—that real—and I have no words to explain how those reactions impacted me. Shame and a sense of absolute ugliness began to crawl over me, and I started walking with my face down to avoid looking at anyone—to look at them was to see my horror in their eyes. People were suddenly coming at me from everywhere, running at me, gaping in disgust. I remember rushing through them to jump into the car and get away as quickly as possible.

Finally we were on our way to the location, a dirt and rock hill on the outskirts of Quarzazate, rising above a rural village named Sigon. Colin and I pulled up, and joined by his assistant, Khadija, we ascended the slope that Bruce Rudnick and I had prayed over the afternoon before. The third assistant director's voice crackled over a distant walkie-talkie, "Bruce/Jesus has arrived and is on his way up."

Now this may sound crazy, but from that point on my memory gets sketchy. I was on top of that hill for probably 12 hours, but I can remember only a handful of specific moments.

You know that point of denial psychologists talk about, where a person experiences something so incredibly traumatic it subconsciously gets blocked from memory? Well, I think that's what happened to me because in the weeks following that day, I couldn't recall too many of its details. My journal shows I was aware of a few specifics and that it was altogether awful, but beyond that, nothing. Then, about five or six weeks later, Bruce and I were together in Cape Town and he showed me a photograph taken that day—"Jesus" falling and the centurions swarming Him. I took one look and started shaking as horror started flooding back to me.

The first horror was stepping over the crest of that hill, arriving on set. The crew was scurrying in preparation with that movie-making excitement crackling through the air. But the second I came into view, tension descended like a black cloud. Making my way through everyone toward Regardt—and I remember this so distinctly—no one said a single word to me. People I'd come to know well walked right by, not even looking at me; yet I could feel their stares from across the hill. They'd glance up, then turn away, shaking their heads in disgust. They were all horrified, and I could feel every look. The drowning in shame and ugliness that swarmed over me—it's a thing I'd never before tasted and am at a loss to explain today, except to say

183

it was awful—just plain awful. The actor who played young Matthew describes the scene in his journal, writing as it was happening:

> When Bruce arrives on set, there is a hushed awe from the crowd. The makeup is unbelievable, showing a Jesus we've never encountered before. Isaiah says He "was marred beyond recognition," and boy have they been faithful to Scripture. His whole nose is a bloodied pulp with pieces of flesh hanging from it; and chunks of beard are missing, exposing bare bone. His eye is virtually closed from battering, and streaks of blood mark his face. It's a horrific sight, and nearby a little girl starts crying.

Aloneness—it's what I remember most about walking through those people—so surrounded, yet so incredibly alone. It swallowed me deeper and deeper with every person that passed. I thank God I didn't see that little girl crying. I wouldn't have been able to handle it.

And the aloneness of hanging on that cross—suspended, helpless to move, abandoned, virtually naked, not even able to scratch an itch or knock a fly off my face; just hanging there, the minutes seeming like hours, people below just staring and not saying a word, some of them crying. It's an aloneness that was beyond my imaginings, and in terms of Jesus, something I'd never considered before but learned very quickly that day.

Jesus, alone. Most everyone He knew and trusted—gone. The whole world staring at His nakedness. Spit and pain, insults and lies, mockery and laughter His only companions. And in that moment, *"Eloi, Eloi, lama sabachthani"*: "My God, my God, why have you forsaken me?" In that moment, as alone as any of us have ever been, none of us have ever been that alone. *Abandoned by the Father*—it's utterly inconceivable. He was so completely alone that day. Jesus.

I remember they found a little wooden chair for me to rest on between setups. It was placed away from the action, and I would sit there by myself as breaks permitted.

While sitting there at one point, I felt something on my left hand. Craning my head around to see out of my one good eye, I saw the little 12-year-old Moroccan girl who had played Jairus' daughter. She was standing next to me, silently holding my hand in hers.

She never said a word but just stood there holding my hand for a good 30 minutes, tears tumbling down her cheeks. She was reaching out to me, caring for me in the only way she knew how, until finally they called me to go back on the cross, and I had to leave.

I can't tell you what that little girl and her simply holding my hand meant in that half hour—to have someone care in the middle of such incredible aloneness. That silent, brave little girl who reached out in such breathtaking innocence—she'll never know all that she meant to me that day. *I'll* never know all that she meant to me.

The very first scene we shot that morning was Jesus and the centurions coming over the hill with cross in tow. We were about ten minutes from a first take when Regardt walked over and told me something that is as humbling as anything I've ever heard.

The night before, we had brainstormed some graphic crucifixion ideas. We wanted to tell the story in its hard realities, and we talked about shot after shot of Jesus going through horror after horror. We were going to give the world what it had never gotten before, and we were excited to give it to them. (Get an actor and a director together and watch the fireworks fly!)

But before the cameras rolled on that first scene, Regardt came bounding up with a mixture of awe and excitement on his face and said, "You won't believe this, but when I was praying about the work this morning, the Lord spoke into my heart: *Don't be sorry for me.*"

Regardt then decided the Lord would have us go ahead and shoot reality, but shoot it simply and honestly, resisting all self-indulgent desires to slap people in the face with it. Consequently all our "tear-squeezer" shots were immediately tossed to the wind.

Another thing was going on that none of the cast or crew was aware of. Beyond the initial scene and two or three others, Regardt wasn't sure what else to shoot even though he had prayed and prayed and then prayed some more. For obvious reasons he didn't share that bit of news with everyone, just myself and probably the other Bruce, but a real behind-the-scenes drama was going. There Reg was, standing on the set with hundreds ready to go at his directive—does he wait for the Lord or take the creative reins in his own hands?

But back to that initial shot. I'm no stuntman, that's for sure, and personally I know of no truly effective way to make a crucifixion look real for the camera outside of actually doing it—especially in light of what the Lord had put on our hearts about filming reality. And on top of that, if you recall, I sensed the Lord had promised me on day one that I wouldn't get hurt. So with all that in mind, I stood ready to do what was necessary to make the shot look great.

There would be no rehearsals. It was one of those shots you just can't rehearse. Beyond setting boundaries and focus marks, mapping specifics would only steal the scene's vitality. We were trying to capture a moment of stark reality, and only stark reality would provide it.

Two cameras would cover the action—one on ground level and one standing above it. A path toward the two was laid for me, and a mark was set where I was to eventually fall. I moved to first position with the crowd and cross behind, and Regardt approached with Moody, his Moroccan assistant director.

Now, without discussion I understood that this was to be shot as documentarily as possible—no pretending. But when the centurions heard this, they got very upset. These fellows were so excited to be "in cinema," but when Moody told them to actually rough me up, their smiles dropped like lead and their north African faces nearly went pale!

I tried to assure them, showing them where to hit me—legs, arms, back, shoulders—spots that could take a hit without real damage yet look effective for camera, but they weren't buying it. They were dying to be in movies, but beating on me just wasn't part of the program. Eventually, however, with some fast talking from Moody, they agreed to give it a go. I remember they were told their attitude was not to be hostility but rather a detached, emotionless, "Let's hurry this thing along so we can get to lunch." If I fell, they were to grab and shove me forward. I was worthless scum to them, and they were to treat me accordingly.

With the centurions agreeable, it was time for final checks. Diana, the costume designer, came and poured fresh streams of blood down the front of my tunic; a crown of very real thorns with the points clipped away was gently fixed atop my head, Regardt stepped behind camera, and every living thing on that hill settled in for take one.

I can't tell you what was in my mind just before Regardt called action that morning—I have no specific memory of it. I do remember being focused, pumped, and keenly aware that these shots were as big as any in the entire film, that this was what it was all about—the cross.

Regardt yelled it—"Action!"—I remember taking maybe three steps when my leg buckled and I went down. Struggling to get up, I fell against a centurion. He gave me a sheepish push into one of the others, I tripped again, and Regardt cut the scene. It wasn't working—the centurions were being much too nice and were much too afraid of hurting me. I got off the ground a little scratched and dirty, Moody gave them a strong talk, and we reset for take two.

From then on it's pretty much a blur. I don't know how many takes we did—five, six, maybe more. I can tell you that somewhere in there the centurions began to take their jobs seriously. I remember being kicked and punched and yanked and mobbed in a cacophony of assault. It was coming at me from everywhere, and I remember going down over and over, and the thorns mashing into my face. I remember tasting real blood in my teeth, and being lifted by the collar, and kicked from behind, and slammed into the dirt. I remember it was awful—to quote my journal, "the absolute subjection/submission to horror."

And somewhere in the middle of all that—and this is a very scary thing to say as well as an impossible thing to explain, as I have no way of knowing exactly what it was that happened or what triggered it— a line of reality was crossed from which there would be no going back the entire day. Somewhere inside of me something snapped in a deep place. Was it in my spirit or in my emotions? Was it the Lord giving me a glimpse of His pain or was it my personal response to being manhandled like I was? I have no way of knowing with certainty. All I can tell you is that it was entirely unexpected, and it was trauma like I never knew trauma could be.

And I began to weep. I would weep the entire day. It was awful beyond awful, and it couldn't have been even a grain of sand on the combined beaches of the universe compared to what Jesus must have gone through 2000 years ago. Khadija, Amina, and all the Moroccan women began to weep as well. I remember them standing in a huddle right of camera, literally sobbing and wailing in each other's arms. Khadija was barking something every time the scene would cut. I couldn't hear what it was, but she was very upset, and I sensed from her gestures that she wanted someone to put a stop to the whole thing.

After every take a host of crew along with the centurions would rush to my aid and help me to my feet—they were all so gentle. Leon, the propmaker, would run in the second Regardt cut the scene and ever-so-carefully lift the thorns off my head, gingerly refixing them for the next shot, waiting till the last second, "Is this okay? Is it too tight? I can loosen it."

I remember Regardt having lengthy discussions with the second unit cameraman, Buster. At dinner that night I discovered what those discussions were about. Buster was so shaken up by what he was seeing through his lens, he felt he couldn't continue. I honestly can't remember whether or not he did. He told Regardt, "What we're doing is wrong" (in the sense of indecent). At dinner he was still saying it.

Regardt later discovered most of the footage Buster shot was useless because his hand was shaking so badly on the camera—and this was a veteran cameraman with many films to his credit as well as years of covering South African political violence for the news. I never talked with him about it, but I have to believe the difference

was that this was Jesus, and the shock of being so confronted with the reality of what He truly went through must have cut Buster to the heart.

Regardt would come and speak to me between every take, but I can't tell you anything he said. He would tell me later that he struggled the entire day about whether or not he should put a stop to what was going on. He said—and I remember his exact words because they so scared me when he spoke them—*"You were going someplace I wasn't sure I could bring you back from."* He thought I was in danger of having some kind of emotional/mental breakdown. I had no idea I was in such bad shape that day, and I'm so thankful the Lord's protective hand was on me through it all because, other than a raw appreciation for what Jesus did for me, I walked away from whatever trauma there was emotionally sound in every way.

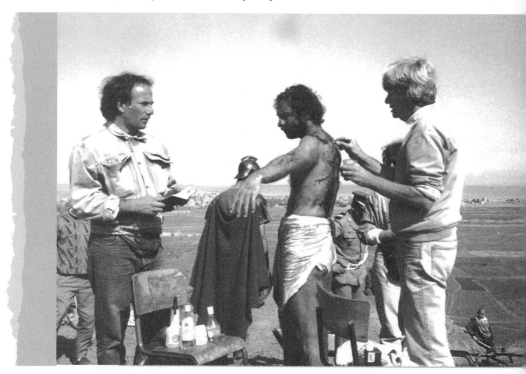

And then there was brother Bruce—my most vivid memory on the day. Through the entire shoot that day, he prayed for me. It wasn't a thing we arranged or discussed—he just did it.

I will never forget hanging on that cross, looking out, and seeing Bruce across the hill, eyes locked onto me, his lips moving in hushed prayer. Over and over I lifted my head seeking that sight, and over and over it gave me the strength to get through the next 30 seconds. And while Diana and Colin touched up my makeup between shots, Bruce stood by my side, his tattered Bible in hand, softly reciting the Messianic prophecies of Isaiah and the Psalms:

> All who see me mock me; they hurl insults, shaking their heads: "He trusts in the Lord; let the Lord rescue him. Let him deliver him, since he delights in him" (Psalm 22:7, 8).
>
> My strength is dried up like a potsherd, and my tongue sticks to the roof of my mouth; you lay me in the dust of death. Dogs have surrounded me; a band of evil men has encircled me, they have pierced my hands and my feet. I can count all my bones; people stare and gloat over me. They divide my garments among them and cast lots for my clothing (Psalm 22:15-18).
>
> I offered my back to those who beat me, my cheeks to those who pulled out my beard; I did not hide my face from mocking and spitting (Isaiah 50:6).
>
> He was despised and rejected by men, a man of sorrows, and familiar with suffering. Like one from whom men hide their faces he was despised, and we esteemed him not (Isaiah 53:3).
>
> He poured out his life unto death, and was numbered with the transgressors. For he bore the sin of many, and made intercession for the transgressors (Isaiah 53:12).
>
> *Jesus*

The second scene we shot that day was Jesus refusing the wine mixed with gall. It started with me sprawled on the ground, the cross lying just out of reach. The centurions were to hoist me to my feet, then jam a wooden bowl in my face, forcing the mixture on me.

My script notes on the day read: "Get back up! I've got to make it!—to the cross. *Drive through the pain!* Keep going—*struggle through the pain.* I *want* to get to the cross despite my failing body: It is my joy—I gotta make it—for my children."

As I mentioned earlier, it was revelation—Jesus wasn't dragged to the cross, He was *crawling to* the cross—His body failing Him, struggling against all odds, a champion pushing through indescribable pain and opposition to see the fulfillment of His mission. Sadly, it got lost in

191

editing, but I remember trying to convey a strong sense of that in this scene.

You see, if He doesn't make it, none of us stands a chance and it all would have been for naught, and He knows that better than anyone. So in spite of the screaming pain and shredded flesh and throat-swelling thirst and draining blood and kicks and blows and spit . . . every inch a mile, every breath a mountain, thrusting Himself forward, straining forward, crawling and dragging Himself forward— *He's got to make it to the cross.*

Face down in the dirt with the cross only a few feet away, Regardt called action, and I reached and dove for it—*as if it was a treasure.* It was just inches from me when the centurions grabbed me by the armpits and yanked me away, slamming that wooden bowl in my mouth as my face twisted and squirmed against it. I remember my legs were buckled beneath me and they just kept jamming that thing into me until finally, mercifully, Regardt yelled, "Cut!"

It was time to change out of my bloodied tunic and into a bloodied loincloth. Then it was over to Colin for another make-up session. He came at me with his "blood" and grime, and started doing to my entire body what he'd done to my face earlier. Diana, the costume designer, went about the same, painting brutal reality all over the loin cloth. This is where Bruce stood with his Bible, softly reading those prophecies, "I offered my back to those who beat me, my cheeks to those who pulled out my beard."

It was in this time of getting painted and smeared and hearing those words that something even deeper inside of me—fathoms deeper—snapped. The memory is so distinct—Colin and Diana were working on me; Diana's assistant was holding a cloak to cut the wind; Bruce was reading; and I looked down. There was "blood" spattered all over my feet and the ground around them. I looked at my left hand, and it was caked under the nails and in the wrinkles of my knuckles. There seemed to be "blood" everywhere, and I guess it was just too real—and I broke.

Colin continued to silently paint me with more and more "blood"—shoulders, back, chest, legs. There was a young British woman there who was supposed to be assisting him, but she couldn't bring herself to get near. She just stood several feet away, staring, completely unable to be of any use. It was just too ugly, too terrible for her.

Bruce continued to read and there was "blood" going everywhere. And then came the moment I looked down at my forearm. Something I should have never done. It was literally covered with the red stuff—I could barely see skin—and it was just too real. I remember shaking and shaking and not being able to stop, and it came over me like water swallowing a drowning man. I just stood there shuddering and sobbing in a state there are no words to describe. And it just got deeper and deeper.

The next scene we shot was the nailing. Lying on the crossbeam, the sun was directly overhead and I remember having to keep my eyes shut against it as the crew worked around me, stepping over me, huddling about me, shifting my body two inches this way, two inches that way. Colin kept spraying me with water to keep me moist, and the centurion kept grabbing my wrist and practicing with the hammer.

Regardt and I had talked earlier about the scene, and he thought Jesus would have been so delirious with pain by this time He may not have even felt the spikes. But I'll tell you, when he called, "Action," and I turned, and this guy had a nail fixed on my hand—I can't tell you the panic that goes through a man's heart when he sees a nail fixed on his hand. And that hammer goes up, and that sound, *Wham!*—there just are no words to describe a thing like that.

Now, if you remember, Regardt wasn't sure how the Lord wanted him to shoot the day. While we were putting down those initial shots, he was working a shade tentatively. But suddenly he was in total command, barking directions like a locomotive in full steam, "Camera goes down here. I want a pan across the crowd ending with the centurion's spear." Somehow, some way, the Lord had laid everything out for him. I remember him prancing over and excitedly telling me about it. You should have seen his face—he was on fire—and with that sureness firmly tucked in his pocket, it was just a matter of knocking each shot out, one by one. He had waited on the Lord, and the Lord had him wait till the last second. But praise God, Reg waited, and I have to believe that was key to the whole thing.

But eventually it was time for me to go up on the cross. I would hang from two leather straps, each secured to an end of the horizontal beam. Leon had fixed a nail head so it would protrude from each strap, and once my hands were jammed inside, Colin would paint them with "blood."

The day before we'd experimented with a hidden seat to make me as comfortable as possible while up there, but that just didn't cut it for purposes of capturing a sense of reality. We tried bringing in a ladder for me to stand on to support myself, but that didn't work either. Regardt and I talked it over and decided it would look best if I was actually hanging while the cameras rolled, so we could get the effect of the neck, arms, and shoulders straining, and of the joints popping. So I'd stand on that ladder, and just before Reg called, "Action," I'd kick off it and drop, literally hanging from my hands with my feet dangling free until the scene was over. Then the crew guys would rush the ladder back under me. I remember Leon grabbing my ankles every time Regardt yelled cut, lifting my body weight as best he could, and guiding my feet to rest on that ladder. It doesn't get any more caring than he was that day.

When there was an extraordinarily long break between shots, they'd take me down for a rest in my little chair, but for the most part I was up there like that the remainder of the day—probably a good nine hours. I will never forget looking out from that cross over the course of those hours and seeing the people weep. Moroccans, crew, cast, spectators—weeping.

There was Kevin, the apostle John. I don't remember if he and I exchanged a single word that day, but the next morning at breakfast he walked into the dining room looking peaked and ill. I was sitting at my plate of fruit and eggs, and he stepped into the doorway moving slowly and carefully with a face that was sour and preoccupied. I thought he'd caught some kind of a bug in the night and asked as he passed, "You feeling okay?" He rested a hand on my shoulder and spoke, "I'm still suffering the repercussions of yesterday."

And Joanna—mother Mary. I will never forget looking down at her from the cross—she was wailing and sobbing in heaves. This was no acting job I was seeing—it was a human being.

Joanna was a tremendous actress, as well as a sophisticated kind of woman. She always came to dinner dressed to the nines and was as skilled at owning a room as she was at owning a scene. But given that sophistication, there was a moment with her while filming that astounds me as much today as when it happened.

It was late in the afternoon, and the sun was beginning to sink. By this time I was more or less out of it—cold, aching, bruised, and spent; just silently hanging, literally counting the seconds till it would all be over. John and the two Marys were huddled beneath me for the shot as the camera crew made final adjustments. I felt something on my feet, bent to see what it was, and could barely believe my eyes. It was Joanna. She was crying, and her arms were clasped around my feet— and she *kissed* them. It was the only way she could think to somehow reach out. I thought I had no more emotions left, but when she did that, I lost it all over again.

But as for my experience on that cross, I remember just hurting all over. As I mentioned, my full body weight was hanging from my hands, which were grasping two leather straps. Those straps were necessarily snug and fit into with great difficulty. I would squeeze my hands as narrow as possible and push through with everything I had while Leon grabbed my fingers from the other side and pulled with everything he had. Because of all that trouble, as well as the extensive makeup needed to cover the whole thing, I'd just leave my hands in those straps between shots unless it was going to be an extraordinarily long wait before the cameras rolled again. A crew member would hold the ladder steady under my feet, and I would just hang while everyone worked around me, moving lights, cameras, and reflector boards.

I remember aloneness beyond aloneness while up there. I remember tasting the warmth of real blood in my teeth from the earlier scenes. I remember being very dry in my throat and mouth, and trying to push moisture up with my tongue. I remember thanking Leon and Colin over and over, though I have no memory of why. And more than anything, I remember brother Bruce sitting on the far side of that hill, eyes locked onto me, lips moving in constant prayer.

We would shoot two lines of dialogue from the cross that day, the first being, *"Eloi, Eloi, lama sabachthani"* ("My God, my God, why have you forsaken me?") There are different theories about this moment in Jesus' life, about exactly what was going on when He cried those words. Some feel He was quoting the Messianic Psalm 22, which begins with the same line, in an effort to call the crowd's attention to the prophecy being fulfilled before them, reaching to the people even in His agony, "Open your eyes! This was prophesied! I am He!" Others feel Jesus was going through a very real tearing apart from God, His Father—that the Father literally turned His back on Jesus in that moment.

What an incomprehensibly devastating thought—to be abandoned by the Father. Think how dark your own alone times have been, yet He was right there. If that's how dark it can feel with Him, can you imagine the darkness without Him? As alone as any of us have felt, not even the most alone has tasted that—the utter blackness of existence without the Father. All talk of horror and agony aside, that's horror and agony unfathomable. My script notes on the scene read very simply: *v. 46—the point of ultimate pain and terror.*

Other than explaining the mechanics for camera, I don't recall whether or not Regardt discussed the scene with me—I was pretty much out of it by this time. I can tell you his scripted directions read:

The look on my face says it all. The soldiers had just dragged me over the hill, and the horror of it all was beginning to hit. I was terrified to do it again, but Leon positions the crown of thorns for another take. Notice the concern of the soldiers and the gentleness of Leon. That's Buster on camera. He was very shaken after this shot.

This is the photo Bruce Rudnick showed me that
released my memory of the events of that day.
I can't tell you the trauma of getting knocked around
by those guys. One of the extras you see to the right
would come to me and say, "I cried for you today."

What strikes me most about this photo is my feet, twisted and contorted. Believe me when I tell you, there was nothing about this that was acting. As you can see, the soldiers were well into their roles by this time.

Joanna Weinberg (Mother Mary) had clearly stopped acting at this point, reacting as a person agonized by what she saw hanging on that cross. Can you imagine what it must have been like for Mary that day 2000 years ago? Mary Magdalene and John grieve as well.

What I was going through that day was trauma like I had never known. The look on my face says it all, as costume designer Diana Cilliers touches up my wardrobe with fresh soil and blood between shots. Just outside of frame, Bruce Rudnick stood reading, "He was pierced for our transgressions, he was crushed for our iniquities; the punishment that brought us peace was upon him."

I can't tell you the panic that goes through a man's heart when he sees a nail fixed on his hand.

"There were many who were appalled at him— his appearance was so disfigured beyond that of any man and his form marred beyond human likeness" (Isaiah 52:14).

And yet He triumphs! Hallelujah! He is risen! My research showed the Greek word at the root of Jesus' "Greetings!" is more literally "It is great to see you!" So that's how we played it. I so love the simplicity, practicality, and down-to-earthness of our Lord. There He is, risen from the dead, one of the two biggest moments in universal history, and He says, "It's great to see you!" I absolutely love it!

> Jesus' face stirs in pain. He draws a breath, weeping, grimacing . . . He screams in agony, incoherently, thrashing about, blood and sweat flying.

Discussion or no discussion, we were obviously thinking along the same lines.

I have to stop here for a minute—it's a little too much for me, sometimes. To look down the throat of those realities, to see those words, to picture Him like that—it's just too much. *Thank You, Jesus, for what You did that day. It's all I've got to offer—thank You.*

Anyway, I remember Regardt was standing alongside the camera on a scaffolding to my left. He told me a shadow would fall across my face, and it was then I was to stir from semiconsciousness and speak the words. If I recall, we rehearsed that shadow once or twice for timing, then it was picture.

I didn't know what I would do when that camera rolled. This was another shot that intimidated me. So many things were going on with Jesus on so many levels. How could I come close to playing even the physical realities, completely aside from the emotional and spiritual? And on a purely practical note, Jesus was moments from death and slipping away. It would have been a tremendous struggle for Him to muster enough consciousness to even give the words voice, let alone speak them with any volume.

Now this may seem a strange thing, but from the cross, just before the camera rolled, I asked for that little Moroccan girl who'd held my hand to be positioned underneath the camera scaffolding, in my eye-line. She just moved me so much I wanted her there, and I can remember it like yesterday—she was standing with her arms by her sides, innocently staring up at me; I looked down at her, and just started to lose it. Then when the camera rolled and that shadow fell, unexplainably I came completely unglued. I wish I could tell you why, but I can't. I can tell you it was a very specific "coming unglued"—it was like being sucked into a vortex of hurt and being helpless to do anything to stop it. I think we shot the scene twice, and the same thing happened both times.

Oh, how awful it must have been for Him that day, 2000 years ago. To feel death start to crawl over Him like that—it must have been just plain awful.

———— ·· ————

Eventually it came time to shoot the death shout—*"And when Jesus had cried out in a loud voice, he gave up his spirit."*

Regardt was on the scaffolding, eye-level to my left. He called action, and I did the scene, my face falling away from him over my right shoulder. After what felt like forever, he softly said, "Cut," then immediately began to give the crew instructions for a second take. I remember he was talking very fast and excitedly, and I rolled my head around to hear what he was saying; and he looked across at me, and his eyes met mine, and he stopped. His face fell—it just dropped—and he stopped. Then he said, "That's it. We're done. Get him down."

I remember telling him, "I can do it again," but he just shook his head and turned to climb down the scaffolding, "No, that's it. We're done." Four or five guys came and took me down from the cross, and it was over. With the exception of a wide silhouette shot, the day was done; the crucifixion was in the books.

Several weeks later Regardt and I were having a cup of coffee together, talking about the day. I looked across the table and asked him why he'd stopped it. I said, "What did you see when you looked at me that made you stop it like that?" Regardt got suddenly very serious and looked away for a long moment. Then he looked back at me and said these words. He said:

I saw a man dying.

Jesus.

There's another scene we shot that day that I haven't yet mentioned. It was a close-up of blood running off Jesus' head, down the thorns, and onto His shoulder. Regardt told me Jesus would be near death in the shot, so it was my job to remain as motionless as possible and allow the blood to run. Colin stood on a ladder to my left, ready to initiate the flow on cue.

My head was down and my eyes closed—I could see nothing. Regardt called action, and after a moment I could feel the red stuff dripping into my hair and down my shoulder. There wasn't a single sound on the entire hilltop—it was as if time itself was standing still.

Suddenly, shattering the intensity, Regardt exploded in excitement, belting at the top of his lungs, "There it is, everyone! There's

your salvation! Take a good look—*the blood of Jesus!* Praise God! There it is! The blood!" He went on and on, thundering in unrestrained worship and thanksgiving.

That was all good and wonderful, but in his ecstasy Regardt forgot about something—*me!* I was hanging up there holding my breath, and as glorious as it was, my arms were tearing and my lungs were about to explode. He was going on and on, and all I could think was, *Cut the scene, Reg! I need to breathe!!*

I'm not so sure he ever did cut the scene—it was all too spectacular and he was all too excited. In fact, if I could have continued holding my breath, I'd probably still be up there today with him dancing circles of wonder up one side of that hill and down the other. But, yes, the blood of Jesus, spilling from His flesh, falling to the ground and staining the dirt, shed for you and me.

A Man dying—*Jesus.*

And why? Why would the Son of the Living God, with all the power of heaven and earth at His fingertips, choose to do a thing like that? The answer is simple, and it's been said time and again. But may its reality wrap around your heart and find a deep, deep home like it never has before.

Because He loves you.
He loves you. He loves you.
Jesus

From December of 1992 through April, 1993—the most remarkable time of my life—I was forced to set aside everything that was my life and take a fresh look at Jesus—someone I assumed I knew well; someone I actually knew very little. And oh, who I discovered—a Man, the Son of the Living God, who was so much more magnificent, so much more extraordinary—so much more Jesus—than I ever dreamed possible. A Man so far beyond my wildest imaginings that with all that's been written in these pages, and the two-and-a-half years it took me to do it, I haven't even come close.

His name was Jesus—the most common name in first-century Israel. Y'shua. The Christ. Messiah. Son of God. Anointed One. Lamb of God. Risen Savior. Rock of Ages. King of Kings and Lord of Lords.

A carpenter's son, born in Bethlehem, raised in Nazareth, killed outside Jerusalem, and resurrected three days later.

Friend, in whatever nation or language you may be reading these words, may we all stop and take a fresh look at Jesus. May we all set our busy worlds aside, stop, and turn our eyes on Him who set His everything aside—His very life—in turning His eyes on us.

Jesus . . . who stretches out a thick, calloused, gentle hand, looks you in the eye, smiles as big as the sun, and says,

> Come to Me. . . . I am gentle and humble in heart,
> and you will find rest for your souls. . . .
> And surely I am with you always,
> to the very end of the age.
> *Jesus*

IS THERE LIFE AFTER "JESUS"?

CHAPTER TWELVE

*I know the plans
I have for you.*

JEREMIAH 29:11

$\mathcal{O}$N THE EVENING OF MAY 1, 1993, Bruce Rudnick and I stood opposite each other with tear-filled eyes in the international terminal of Jan Smuts Airport, Johannesburg, South Africa. I was moments away from boarding a Swissair jet bound for Los Angeles, leaving behind both him and Regardt, along with the entire *Matthew* adventure.

After we wrapped the film, Regardt took his family to Botswana for a holiday, and Bruce and I got on a bus that would take us into the bushveldt for rest, wildlife, solitude, and prayer. We stretched our time together as far as we could out there, and it was wonderful, but as we stood in that airport facing each other, the clock had finally run out. It was time to say goodbye.

My heart was clinging to South Africa, but I'd prayed and felt certain the Lord wanted me to return to L.A. So there I was, bag in hand, sharing silent tears with my dear brother, facing what neither of us wanted to face.

The adventure was over. *Matthew* had ended. All that lingered was the long hair, the beard, and a treasure-trove of experiences that had radically altered my life, as well as the lives of many others.

At that moment Regardt, Bruce, and I faced uncertain futures. Regardt and Bruce had both moved their families cross-country from Johannesburg to Cape Town, believing that *Matthew* was the first step in a career of filming all 66 books of the Bible for the Cape Town-based production company, but that was far from assured. As for me, I was on my way home, where life was exactly where I'd left it three months earlier.

It was a scary time—all any of us truly had was Jesus—and as I hugged my brother goodbye, feeling his heart pound out of his chest for me to stay, I was fueled singularly by the Lord's Jeremiah 29:11 promise of "a future and a hope." That was the only thing pushing my feet through customs and toward Swissair 375.

I was leaving behind the consummate coming together, fulfillment, and expression of everything my life was about personally and professionally. Ultimate purpose, ultimate fellowship, ultimate use of passions and talents, and all of it wrapped in the ultimate adventure—walking in the sandals of Jesus. I'd been to the mountain, and I knew it. We'd all been to the mountain, and we all knew it.

Never will I forget whispering to the Lord as I stared out the window of that jet into the African sky, in honesty and complete fullness of mind, "Lord, I've lived life like I never dreamed possible in the last three months. I can't imagine anything that could top it. If this plane goes down with me in it, I want You to know I'm smiling all the way."

And I meant that. Brother Bruce, the consummate encourager, was always quoting the Word to me as well as himself, "He promises to take us from glory to glory, my bru—glory!" But as nice as that was to hear, and as much as I smiled and nodded, I honestly could think of nothing that could ever come close, outside of returning to Quarzazate and doing it all over again. Deep inside, as brave as we all tried to be, none of us could.

But the Lord is so full of surprises, and I have a feeling when He hears me say things like that, He just laughs, "You're thinking so small, kid. You think on this level, but I'm thinking on THIS LEVEL," as His mighty hands stretch as wide as the universe. "Just you wait and see, kid. Just you wait and see."

I had a dream in the months after returning home. It was a wonderful dream—the most wonderful I've ever had. I can't say for sure it was a dream from the Lord, though I hope with all my heart it was. It went like this—

Regardt and I were in an open jeep, driving along a dirt road, cutting through the middle of a vast expanse of open land—nothing but land as far as the eye could see in every possible direction. I was at the wheel, and Regardt was sitting in the backseat.

We pulled up to a definite, thick black line intersecting the road and stretching to both horizons. I stopped, climbed out of the jeep, and the Lord spoke to me, "This line is your border. You draw your other border."

Looking over the expanse, I thought, *Well, I'll take a little bit, here,* and started to draw a parallel line in the sand just a few feet from the other. Then I stopped and boldly proclaimed, "What am I doing? I'll take more!" I walked about 20 feet further and started to draw a second line. But then I stopped again, "I can't take that much. Who do I think I am? I'll just take a little sliver." I stepped back to a thin margin and began again, only to stop again.

I went back and forth like that several times, trying to decide how much to take, getting more and more frustrated with myself, not knowing what to do. Finally I spun around to Regardt and said, "I can't figure out what to do, Reg. Will you draw my other border for me?"

Without a single word or moment's hesitation, Regardt jumped out of the jeep and ran down the road. He ran, and he ran, and he ran . . . farther, and farther, and farther . . . till he was nothing more than a pinpoint dot on the horizon, having run as far as a straining eye could possibly see. Then he stopped, turned, and began to draw my other border.

End of dream. Like I said, I sure hope it was from the Lord.

A few weeks after I left South Africa, Reg and I sat in a coffee shop in L.A. He'd flown out to film the narrated "old Matthew" segments with Richard Kiley in the hills of Malibu, and we sat sipping what was probably our fifteenth cup of java, talking the whole thing over.

The sun was setting outside, and cars were streaming by on the highway below us. Regardt looked me in the eye and said, "God doesn't give you an experience like you had just to let you go, Bruce. This is just the beginning. I'm telling you, the plane hasn't even gotten off the ground—it's still sitting on the runway. I'm telling you, brother; I'm telling you."

That sounded great, but after he returned to Cape Town the California months that followed were some of my longest. I wandered through each day one mixed-up guy, struggling to somehow get on with the business of living "real life."

One night I was back playing for my old softball team. There I was at my usual shortstop position, but just standing there in a daze, my mind thousands of miles away (literally). Ground balls were whizzing by me left and right, and I just stood watching them roll into the outfield. It must have looked hilarious (to everyone but my teammates, of course).

Between innings the first baseman came jogging over and asked, "Are you okay, Bruce?"

"Sure, why?"

"You look like a guy who went to heaven, and God said, 'Your time isn't up yet; you have to go back,' and He sent you back down to earth."

This guy wasn't even a believer, and he had me pegged perfectly. That's exactly how it felt inside—like I'd gone to heaven and been sent back to earth and forced to deal with it.

As for the professional side of things, I just plain had no idea who I was anymore or what my life was all about. I'd left Los Angeles an ambitious actor who knew the Lord and returned a man desperately in love with Jesus, a man having tasted in His life the way life was truly meant to be lived, but without the slightest clue of what to do with it all.

On top of that, after the employment drought of '92 and being out of town for the first quarter of '93, it seemed I had only a shadow of a career remaining. And that tore my heart up, because, along with all the excitement for Jesus, I'd also walked away from *Matthew* with a new excitement for making movies. I remember feeling that excitement explode and multiply with every hour we were working. Knowing the future was a question mark, it was dangerous to give place to that, so I begged the Lord constantly, "Lord, if *Matthew* is all my being an actor is about, please take that passion out of my heart." But He didn't—quite the contrary, in fact. I walked away from the whole adventure with a thousand times more passion for making movies than before.

So there I was—heart aching all over the place, lost in an experience I didn't know what to do with—dying to return to the fellowship, adventure, and purpose I had known; homesick for a South Africa that wasn't home and friends I'd only known a few months; screaming to get back on the set, but having no set to get back to.

And there was one more thing—and this was a big, big thing. It's difficult to put into words, but I remember feeling something of a "freak" much of the time. I would sit in conversation after conversation and gathering after gathering, and as hard as I tried, it seemed so difficult to participate. I remember having a hard time relating to people or even enjoying other people's company, always feeling like a square peg in a sea of round holes.

That was especially exaggerated with people who didn't know the Lord. I'd be sitting there and they'd be talking away, having the greatest time, and my heart would just be ripping. Often I'd have to excuse myself and go outside or sit in the car.

As a result, I found myself becoming somewhat withdrawn. I'm sure folks around me had a hard time understanding why, and I probably didn't do too good a job explaining it to them. Neither could people figure out why I couldn't seem to leave *Matthew* behind and jump right back into the Hollywood machinery. For years they'd been watching me live and die for a television series, but now they could sense that something was very different. They didn't know what it was or how to deal with it, and I couldn't figure it out myself, let alone include anyone in it. So to say the least, it was an awkward time for all concerned, and I thank God for my family's and friends' patience during it.

But consequently, I spent most of that summer alone, whether it was swimming at the beach, or walking my dog, or jogging the streets around my home, or just sitting in a coffee shop. I spent many hours every day—quite often entire mornings and afternoons—in prayer and reading the Word. I did a lot of searching, a lot of seeking, a lot of trying hard to put it all together and somehow get on with living life. I remember several times getting out of bed in the middle of the night—three, four o'clock in the morning—taking my dog to the park and talking with the Lord for hours. I would sit on the swing and throw Chub his tennis ball, or sometimes I'd just walk around and he would chase squirrels. Some of those nights we'd be out till well after sunrise.

But there was a spark of light at the end of the tunnel, and my eyes were solidly locked onto it. *Matthew* was soon to be released in South Africa, and the producers had asked me to return for a promotional tour. Aside from all the praying, it was that anticipation that carried me through the summer, and on October 10, 1993, I was staring out the window of a 747, looking down upon my beloved Cape Town and smiling so big my face almost split up the middle.

It was to be a whirlwind tour, taking me into every corner of the country, sharing *Matthew* stories with the South African people. Airplanes, hotels, churches, newspapers, magazines, dignitaries, schools, radio, television—the whole ball of wax. It was to be my life for the next five weeks.

The first step was a bit of a shock. I walked off that jet and into a terminal full of reporters, photographers, fans, and schoolchildren—there was even an orchestra playing for me! I was expecting only a few good friends and a quiet hamburger in the airport cafe, so, to say the least, I was a little shocked (and somewhat embarrassed as well). The next morning, eating breakfast in the hotel restaurant, there was a huge photo of me in the newspaper. Looking at that photo and reading the story that went with it, I just had to laugh over the incredible ironies of my life. Just 48 hours before I was watching my dog chase tennis balls, and here I was on the front page of a national newspaper. It seemed so crazy.

But the Lord is so clever—as I sat laughing at myself that morning, little did I know that a brand-new adventure was about to begin. Little did I know that what Regardt had spoken to me in Los Angeles so many months before—"God doesn't give you an experience like you had just to let you go"—was about to come true. Little did I know that God was planning to do something so far beyond anyone's imagination, to this day I still look back on it and shake my head in wonder.

It all started in a city named Bloemfontein. We had traveled to a handful of places by that time, averaging probably four meetings a day. Everywhere we went, I could see the Lord moving people to new excitement and freshness in Him. He was touching lives in every way, but something extraordinary happened in that little city whose name I'd never heard before—something beyond extraordinary.

I was scheduled to speak to an assembly of students and faculty at one of the country's most prestigious high schools, Grey College. Approaching the platform, I beheld a virtual sea of young men identically dressed in their traditional white shirt, tie, and striped blazers. It was a foreign sight to my American eyes, and somewhat intimidating in its formality.

I talked with the students for about 15 minutes following a film clip of *Matthew*, then sat down in the far corner of the stage. I don't recall what stories I told—it was early in the morning and there were four more engagements ahead of me, so I'm sure the only thing going through my mind was, *Okay—that's one down, four to go.*

A man in a suit (he may have been the school chaplain) took the platform following me and addressed the teenagers in their native language. A guy sitting to my right leaned over to me and whispered a translation. This man in the suit was inviting the high schoolers to commit their lives to Jesus. He kept gesturing a beckoning wave, referring to the final *Matthew* scene where Jesus turns and invites the viewers to follow Him.

The invitation was a shock—I had no idea he was going to do it. It had been done in a few church settings after I spoke, but here we were in a high school assembly, and it took me completely by surprise. Whoever this guy was, he said to the students, "If you believe these things in your heart, and you want to ask Jesus into your life, then stand up." *Instantaneously*, without a moment's hesitation, *800* young men sprang to their feet.

I couldn't believe my eyes—no one could. The guy was so amazed he told them all to sit back down, then went on to explain the whole thing to them again. This time, however, he told them not to stand because their friends were standing, or because their teachers were watching, but only if they seriously wanted to make this lifechanging commitment. He made it very hard for them, then gave a second invitation. Astoundingly, the same 800 immediately stood up. In the utter silence blanketing the room in that moment, the guy next to me whispered, "How's that for salvation?"

By the end of that morning, in three similar meetings in the same auditorium, more than 2000 young people stood to the same invitation. We walked out speechless, and driving away, sitting silently in the backseat, it hit me: *God is doing far more here than promoting videos.*

That day my tour turned into a full-blown ministry. When the five weeks ended, I was neck-deep in invitations to speak at everything from prisons, orphanages, and mental institutions to holiday caravan parks; from Robben Island to the Kalihari Desert; and from the war-torn townships of Khayelitsha and Mamelodi to the offices of Nobel Peace Prize winners F.W. DeKlerk and Bishop Desmond Tutu.

In response to those invitations, I would remain in South Africa for five months beyond that five-week tour. My constant companions would be airplanes, hotel rooms, suitcases, and microphones. I would travel back and forth across the country countless times, averaging three or four meetings a day, six and seven days a week. I would see families reunited, marriages redeemed and restored, racial walls crumbled to the ground, satanists delivered, a woman healed of cancer, and thousands of people from every imaginable corner of society discover Jesus.

Yes, Regardt had spoken truth. The life-transformation in front of my eyes in those months was so stunning, so whirlwind a display of the love of God poured on His kids, that to this day I have yet to comprehend even a fraction of all that it was.

That adventure would eventually come to an end as well, though my final ministry chapter is far from being written. I've returned to South Africa often since then, God doing the same magnificent things each time. And seeds of the same are fast sprouting on this side of the ocean as well. It's a thrilling thing, for sure, and I pray it continues to grow and grow.

I haven't made any movies since *Matthew*, other than a few relatively small jobs. But I'm confident of those talents, excited to get back in action, and feeling strongly that the Lord is far from done with me in that vocation.

Of course, it goes without saying that my dream is to film all the Gospels just as we did *Matthew*. Regardt, Bruce, and I long for that day when we will again stand side by side on location in Quarzazate. Our collective hearts ache for that opportunity. It's our greatest passion and desire.

But all of these hopes and dreams and longings are completely in the Lord's hands. There's nothing I can do, really, to make any of them go, other than lay them at His feet in prayer, trust Him, look for the doors He opens, and step through. In fact, from a purely human standpoint, sitting here in Los Angeles penning these final words, it all looks like a barrelful of impossibilities.

But then I remember a Quarzazate day when I strolled a palm tree-lined path dressed in a robe and sandals, flanked by a scruffy band of ragtag disciples. Regardt called, "Action," I threw my hands up in praise to the Father, spun around to the crowd behind me, and joyfully exclaimed:

With God, all things are possible!

And then I look back even further to a cold morning in 1992 in a tiny North Hollywood house, when I stood watching the rain through an open window, examining every corner of my life and concluding, *It's all impossible.* As I had no idea then what God would do with that "impossible," I must look forward in confidence toward what He will undoubtedly do with this "impossible." I hope with all that I am, He's looking down at me right now with that huge smile of His, and saying, "Just you wait, kid. You ain't seen nothin' yet. Just you wait."

And so I wait—and pray; as does Regardt; as does Bruce. And I do the only thing I can do; the smartest thing I can do; the most productive, most exciting, most sure thing I can do—in fact, it's the only thing any of us can do:

> . . . fix our eyes on Jesus,
> the author and perfecter of our faith,
> who for the joy set before him endured the cross,
> scorning its shame. . . .

> Consider *him*, who endured such opposition
> from sinful men.

> *Jesus.*

I love You, Lord. I don't understand much, but I know that I love You, and my life is in Your hands—that I know for sure.

Whatever You've got in mind for tomorrow, Lord, if I even have a tomorrow, I look forward to it. And though it doesn't seem possible, I look forward to it being just as remarkable, if not more, than what's gone before because that's just the kind of God You are.

And thanks for all You did for me—not just in making the movie, but in Your life—the cross and everything. Yes, Lord, thanks for the cross.

You really are something special, you know—something really special.

Bruce

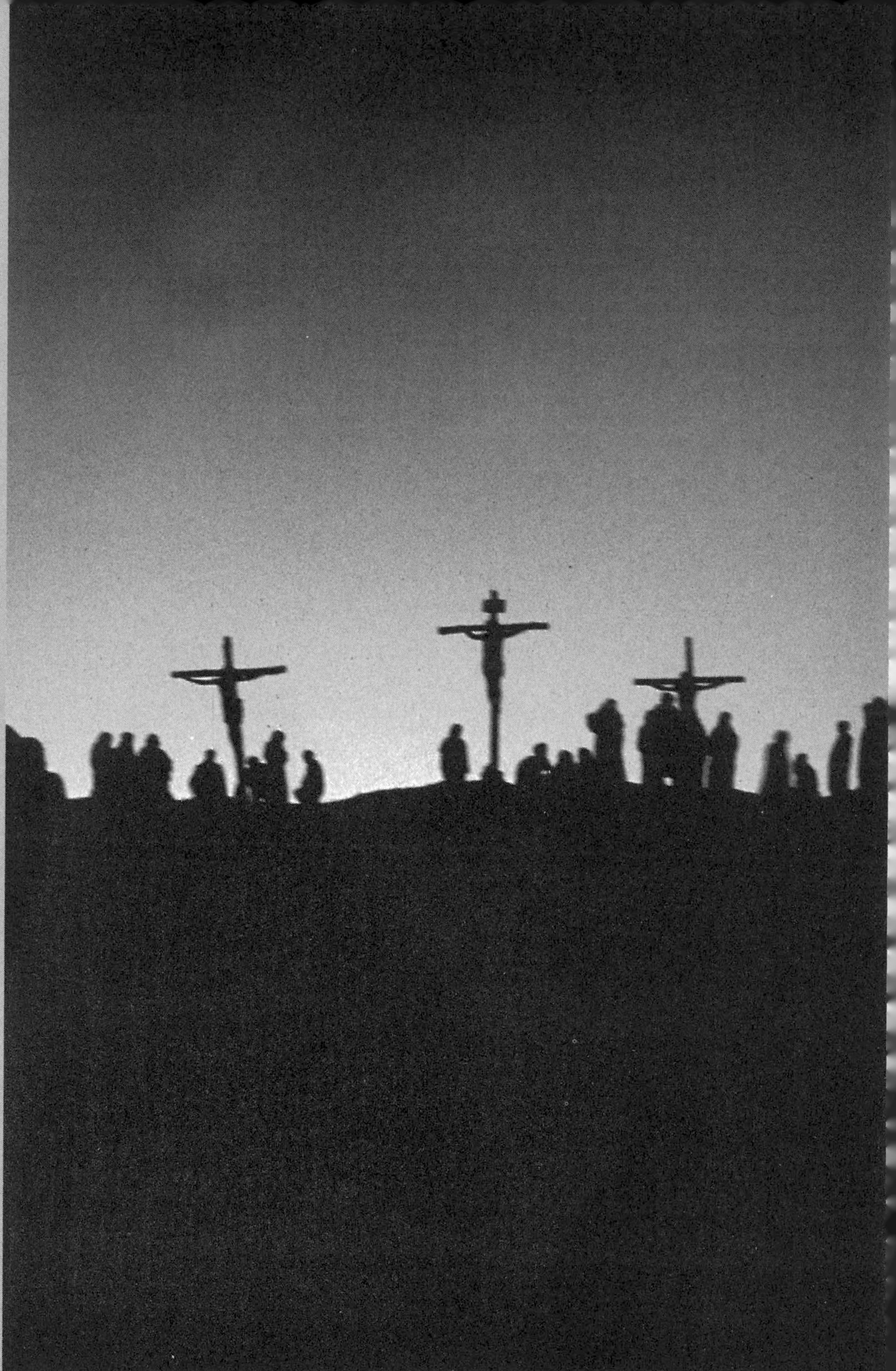

A CALL TO RESPONSE

For all have sinned and fall short of the glory of God.

ROMANS 3:23

The wages of sin is death, but the gift of God is eternal life in Christ Jesus our Lord.

ROMANS 6:23

God demonstrates His own love for us in this; while we were still sinners, Christ died for us.

ROMANS 5:8

Everyone who calls on the name of the Lord will be saved.

ROMANS 10:13

I HAVE NO IDEA WHERE YOU MAY BE IN YOUR LIFE TODAY. Chances are, if you've gotten this far in this book, you've already begun some kind of relationship with Jesus. That is, you've come to a point of recognizing the truth of those Scriptures above and made a decision in your heart to believe them, to trust Jesus in them, to found your salvation and live your life in them—and that's fantastic. But on the outside chance you haven't made that kind of decision, I'd be doing you a great disservice if I closed without offering you the opportunity to do so.

The Word of God says (and don't take my word for it but always check for yourself), "For God so loved the world that he gave his one and only Son, that whoever believes in him shall not perish but have eternal life" (John 3:16). And then there's what Jesus Himself said— "I am the way and the truth and the life. No one comes to the Father except through me" (John 14:6).

Remember the story about Jesus crying in heartbreak on the temple steps in Jerusalem: "How often I have *longed* to gather your children together, as a hen gathers her chicks under her wings, but you were not willing" (Matthew 23:37)? If you haven't come to a place of decision for Jesus, He weeps for you today just as He did for those people 2000 years ago. It's true—He loves you, and His heart is *for* you, to forgive, and give His life, and welcome you into His Father's kingdom. And that welcome is for all, no matter how unforgivable or unwelcomable you may feel you are or may have been falsely told you are. His salvation is *complete* and *final* and *eternal* and *available*—to you—free for the asking. It is the free gift of eternal life (Romans 6:23) bought and paid for by His death on the cross and guaranteed by His resurrection from that death.

Maybe you're a person who's been sitting in churches your whole life or maybe you're a person whose life has been so void of God it isn't funny—I don't know. All I know is your salvation is in Him, and it comes by an act of faith in a moment of decision. If you've never in your life made that decision, the time to do so is now. So I ask you, *Where do you stand with the God who created you?* Only you and He know.

I like to tell the high school kids, "Jesus is very cool. He doesn't force Himself on anyone. He just stands outside the door of your heart and knocks, 'May I come in? May I give you a hand with those things and help you get through life? May I give you eternal life? May I love you? Look at the nail holes in my hands and try to tell me I don't love you. Do you believe I'm for real—that I lived and died— and that My death is your salvation unto eternal life with Me and My

Father? Do you believe I rose from the dead and live today, the Son of the Living God? Do you believe it—do you want it? Not just in your head, but in your heart, in your gut. Tell Me, *Who do you say I am?*'"

Only you know if the Lord is knocking on the door of your heart right now, and only you can open it. If you believe in your heart and right now want to open that door and say, *Yes, Jesus, I believe. I choose You. I want You.* If you want to receive His love and live in His embrace; if you want to live in the hope of eternal life—then just tell Him. Tell Him right where you are, right now. I guarantee He hears you. *Jesus, I'm a sinner. Forgive me. I need You. Come.*

There are no magic words, no fancy prayers, no ceremonies or rituals. Just tell Him what's in your heart. Be honest with Him—He knows your every thought, feeling, struggle, confusion, and worry—you can't hide a thing from Him, so just be honest. *Jesus, I don't know too much right now, but I believe You're real, and I believe You died for my sins, and I'm trusting You to forgive me and be my Savior. In the best way I know how, I open my heart to You—come in and make me new in You. Amen!*

Now go and tell someone you trust about the decision you've made—maybe someone you know who really loves Jesus. That open step of commitment is an important thing. Get yourself a Bible and start getting to know Jesus—the title of that Book should be *This Is Who I Am*, by Jesus Christ. Read the Psalms and the book of John. Talk with the Lord—pray. Talk with Him about everything—He wants to be a part of your *everything*.

Find a good, challenging, loving, Bible-teaching church. He doesn't want any of us to go it alone, and a good church will help you to grow in Him. Keep in mind that no group or church is going to be perfect—and if you ever come across one that claims it is or pretends to be, run out of there as fast as your feet can take you!

And so important—check everything you hear against the Word of God. There are many misleading preachers running around, but as long as you check what you hear to make sure it matches what you see in the Word, you won't get into trouble.

Keep in mind it doesn't mean your life is suddenly going to be wonderful or you'll never make another mistake. Life is life, and none of us is perfect, and the same problems you had two minutes ago will still be facing you an hour from now. The big difference is you've now got the God who made heaven and earth to guide and pull you through whatever it may be; and your hope is now in eternal life with Him and not in ever-fluctuating circumstances.

Cast *all* your cares upon Him—He loves to heal, renew, redeem, and resurrect—it doesn't matter what it is, how big or small. Sometimes He does it in a moment, and sometimes He takes His time, but He guarantees He "will *never* leave you nor forsake you," and "I know the plans I have for you . . . plans to prosper you and not to harm you, plans to give you hope and a future."

I commit you to His care and pray blessing and goodness and the fullness of all you were created to be in your life, now and forever—in the name of Jesus. Amen!

Wow! I can't tell you how big a deal that is to Jesus for you—one of His kids—to come to Him. I'm telling you, the angels in heaven are dancing in joy and having a big-time party for you right now. I wish I were there to see it!

But you know, like I said, chances are you made that decision in your life some time ago and have already begun a walk with Jesus. It might be a strong walk or it might be a weak one, but at least it's begun, and that's the important thing.

My own walk these days has been difficult. Lately I've been beleaguered by the pressures of life's struggles, and so profoundly aware of my own sin nature, and how there is no righteousness in me whatsoever outside of Jesus Christ. It isn't a nice thing to face, but He and He alone is the sole reason I can get through a day without giving in to the junk of life. I don't know if I've ever been more aware of how desperately I need Jesus than I am right now.

But wherever you may be in your life, brother; wherever you may be, sister; whatever mess you may think you've made or however wonderful you may feel you are—take a moment, get on your face before Him, and thank Him. He did a lot for you, you know; and He loves you. He loves you so much.

Jesus

AUDIO BOOK

Available from your local
Christian bookstore

ISBN 1-56507-796-2

When actor Bruce Marchiano landed the role of Jesus in *The Gospel According to Matthew,* he knew God's hand had led him to this turning point. But he never imagined the life-changing experiences that lay ahead.

Come with Bruce on this intensely personal journey as he walks in the foosteps of Jesus. From the joy of healing a beloved child to the emotional isolation and physical devastation endured on the cross to the triumphant reality of the resurrection, you'll experience an intimate glimpse into the heart of God.

As Bruce speaks honestly from his heart, you'll hear awe mixed with the joy and humor of one man's testimony in the hands of God. This audio book comes complete with background music and actual audio excerpts from the film.

Other Good Books by Bruce Marchiano

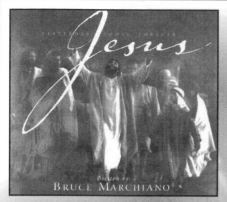

Jesus Yesterday, Today, Forever

What was it like 2000 years ago? What was it *really* like?

Come! Hear the shofar's trumpet call to worship echoing across the hills and valleys of ancient Israel. There's talk of a new prophet—a carpenter from the town of Nazareth in Galilee.

Stand in the temple courts with Him, share a meal by His campfire. Laugh with Him, weep with Him. Look into His heart, and glimpse the very liberation of your soul—

This beautiful book includes more than a hundred pages of stunning, full-color photography and moving text.

Jesus—An Audiodrama

The unforgettable story of Jesus springs to life with music, special effects, and dramatic reading by actor Bruce Marchiano. Share a meal with Jesus by His campfire. Hear His voice. Sense the warmth of His embrace. Laugh with Him, weep with Him, feel the heartbreak of His death and triumph of His resurrection.

Available at your local Christian bookstore